AMY WINEHOUSE

THE BIOGRAPHY

CHAS NEWKEY-BURDEN

JB

JOHN BLAKE

Published by John Blake Publishing Ltd,
3 Bramber Court, 2 Bramber Road,
London W14 9PB, England

www.johnblakepublishing.co.uk

First published in paperback in 2009

ISBN: 978-1-84454-720-1

British Library Cataloguing-in-Publication Data:
A catalogue record for this book is available from the British Library.

Design by www.envydesign.co.uk

Printed in Great Britain by CPI Bookmarque, Croydon, CR0 4TD

1 3 5 7 9 10 8 6 4 2

Text copyright © Chas Newkey-Burden, 2008

Photos courtesy of Rex Features, Empics/PA Photos, Getty Images and Matrix Photos

Papers used by John Blake Publishing are natural, recyclable products made from wood grown in sustainable forests. The manufacturing processes conform to the environmental regulations of the country of origin.

CONTENTS

Acknowledgements

I'd like to thank all those who granted me time for interviews, including Julie Burchill, Garry Mulholland, Paolo Hewitt, Mark Simpson and Zeddy Lawrence.

Thanks to Stuart Robertson and John Blake for the deal. To Andy Armitage for copy-editing, Amy McCulloch for easing the book to paperback and to Diana Colbert and Rosie Ries for always being brilliant.

Thanks to David J Brown for his "Ahhhs" and Katie Glass for her tip-offs. I am always grateful to my friends who encourage and inspire me, including Lucian Randall and the wonderful Frankie Genchi of fleckingrecords.co.uk.

Finally, thanks to Chris for everything.

The author blogs at www.newkey-burden.com

PREFACE

It was when Amy Winehouse learned that during a meeting of the United Nations she had been held responsible for African poverty that she knew she had heard it all. For so long, this talented singer had been an obsession for the tabloid press and had learned to live with their relentless glare. However, when Antonio Maria Costa, head of the United Nations Office on Drugs and Crime, singled her out, saying she glamorised drug use and was thus 'causing another disaster in Africa', she must have wondered if the world had gone mad.

The report came at a busy time in Amy's life – a period of activity that was in turn weird, wonderful and woeful. The media, of course, were there to document every moment of it. She called her audience 'monkey c**ts' during a shambolic performance in Birmingham, and, that same evening, a cross-dressing stalker was ejected from the venue, despite his pained insistence he could look after her while her husband was incarcerated. Most reporters and fans had little good to say about the show; it was left – somewhat bizarrely – to Andrew Lloyd Weber and David Frost to defend her, insisting as they did that the performance had many merits. To add to the surreal atmosphere, Lloyd Webber went on to write an open letter to Amy in the pages of *Hello!* magazine.

Not that the musical maestro's support meant the media were about to turn the temperature down on Amy. One newspaper claimed some burnt foil was thrown from her tour bus and another asked, 'Is it impolite to ask if you've been to powder your nose, Amy?' after she was photographed with a white circle inside her nostril. By the time a video clip of a recent concert surfaced on the Internet showing her retrieve something from her beehive and move it towards her nose, nobody seemed interested in admitting that, studied properly, the footage seemed to show her doing nothing more sinister than wiping her nose with a tissue.

Soon, she was causing raised eyebrows in the air. 'Our famous little friend is smoking in the toilet,' meowed a sour air hostess during Amy's flight to Scotland. Naturally, raised voices were heard as the singer jostled her way through the airport. News that her tour manager had quit did little to calm matters and before long her family were showing their increasing concern. Her brother Alex surfaced on television, telling the GMTV viewers that Amy was fine and then, after she returned to the capital, her parents called an ambulance to her home in the early hours after she had disappeared. A sick rumour shot across the Internet that the twenty-four-year-old had died of a drug overdose.

However, Amy was alive and receiving help and plaudits from all manner of people. Cheryl Cole of Girls Aloud spoke of Amy's talent; Duran Duran's Simon Le Bon said he wanted to give her a good feed and admitted he was worried about her breasts. (Wild boy!) Then, rockers Queens of the Stone Age paid tribute to her live on stage. Her notoriety was becoming truly global. No wonder she was voted the 'Most Buzzed About Star' by a leading American entertainment magazine.

Back on stage, Amy was dedicating songs to her imprisoned husband Blake. 'I can only phone him before or after *EastEnders*,' she told her audience during an insightful mood. Away from the shows, she signed up for yoga lessons and chuckled when she learned that controversial *Big Brother* star Jade Goody and her fella had done a photoshoot dressed up as Amy and Blake. It didn't look half as ridiculous as one might have thought. Finally, the media reported with some shock the tumultuous news that Amy had got a taxi home after a concert in Brighton. 'It was really strange,' said a shaken eyewitness. Hold the front page!

From being blamed for poverty in Africa to her shock-horror south-coast taxi stunner, via burnt foil, Simon Le Bon and so much more, it had been a busy week in the land of Amy.

INTRODUCTION

She told us she was trouble, but we know that she's so good. Amy Winehouse is one of the most talented, honest and newsworthy artists ever to emerge from the UK music scene. She has sold millions of records, won numerous awards and won critical respect from all ages, tastes and fanbases. Her songwriting skills and rich, soulful voice make her stand head and shoulders above the competition. However, in recent years Amy has become known less for her beautiful voice and wonderful songs than for her hedonistic, controversial lifestyle.

In one of her songs, Amy sings of dying a hundred times. She has certainly had more than her fair share of lives already. At just twenty-four years of age, the dynamic diva had won more musical awards, sparked more tabloid headlines and written more memorable, classic songs than most artists could hope to in a lifetime. Yes, her profile and success have often come at a price but, while that has sometimes been uncomfortable for her, for those who choose to read a book about her life story it is a happier prospect, promising as it does a story full of drama and incident.

Amy's musical image defies stereotyping or pigeonholing. Her music, which was in the early days steeped firmly in the jazz tradition, has become an increasingly multifaceted affair, taking in funk, soul, R&B and hip-hop among many other genres. Just as her music defies pigeonholing, so does her wider image. In any given week, Amy can be plastered over the front page of a tabloid newspaper for her latest rumoured indiscretion, photographed in a celebrity weekly leaving a bar, have her music discussed in music weeklies and also be chewed over as a cultural icon in the pages of broadsheet newspapers and during highbrow chattery on posh radio stations. She is, all-round, a glorious mass of contradictions. As renowned music critic Garry Mulholland put it, Amy 'Sounds Afro-American: is British-Jewish. Looks sexy: won't play up to it. Is young: sounds old. Sings sophisticated: talks rough. Musically mellow: lyrically nasty.'

Her producer, Mark Ronson, expands on Amy's multifaceted nature. 'I've had the luxury of working with someone like Amy Winehouse, who's such an iconic figure and makes it sound modern,' he says. 'Anyone else might have made it sound like some sort of retro pastiche.' His assessment is, unsurprisingly, spot on. Her sound may be rooted firmly in traditional jazz and soul from deep back in the twentieth century, but the subjects of her songs have distinctly twenty-first-century themes: footballers' wives, rehab, Beastie Boys T-shirts. As for Amy, she has described herself as everything from being 'very maternal' to 'an ugly dickhead drunk'.

Then there is contradiction of her stage performances. First there is the supreme confidence: witness the proud, almost sneering expression she pulls during the opening *a capella* line of 'Me and Mr Jones'. Yet she can also appear enchantingly vulnerable and uncomfortable on stage, forever readjusting her dress and – of course – often taking to the stage after more than a few drinks, surely a sign of nerves as well as any wider issues.

LA Weekly, writing up a concert she gave on the Sunset Strip, wrote,

> What was especially interesting about the performance was the way Winehouse handled her nerves – besides frequent sips taken from a cup at the edge of the stage. She stared down at the stage a lot, then looked up with a sneer or curled lip that evoked gum-popping, eyeball-rolling femmes from Ronettes to B-girls, gangsters' molls to biker chicks. But there were also fleeting moments when she clearly checked out of her own performance: Her eyes would simply go blank, and she'd retreat behind them. Still, that voice – the sound of mysteriously missing teeth, Spanish Harlem stoops in summer and declarations of undying love – never wavered, and was never less than amazing.

Her true fans lap up all her contradictions, good and bad. Rarely has there been a more supportive fanbase than that enjoyed by Amy. She might sing a song about being just friends, but her relationship with her real fans is true love, despite reports of disgruntled fans at her winter 2007 UK tour.

She has successfully reinvented her image, too. When she first stepped under the spotlight, Amy was a young, fresh-faced Jewish princess. A protégée of *Pop Idol* guru Simon Fuller, she had a voice beyond her years and was pleasingly curvy and well behaved. Well, comparatively well behaved. Then, after her first album was released, Amy disappeared off the radar. She then returned as a slimmer, cooler and decidedly darker star. Covered in tattoos with a huge beehive and an unpredictable nature, she was a million miles from her former self. When a television host told her how much he had liked and got along with the 'first' Amy during his interviews with her on Channel 4's *Popworld*, she laughed and said, 'She's dead.'

But is the old Amy *really* dead? 'I'm a nice girl,' she protests. 'Everyone says I'm a bitch, but, like the stuff in the papers, it's only the bad stuff. It's not going to make the papers if I cook dinner for twelve of my best friends and we have a lovely night doing nothing but talking and laughing, know what I mean?

'That's really the kind of person I am. I'm just a little Jewish housewife really. It's just that I'm working so much at the moment that it's hard for me to look after my baby,' she said, referring to her then boyfriend. 'I had my first day off for so long the other day and all I did was stay home and cook all day for my boyfriend, my family, my dad, my manager, clean the house. That's what I like to do.'

If a single song sums up the new Amy, it is, of course, 'Rehab'. Here she was at her defiant, controversial and most outspoken best. Her first album might have been called *Frank* – in reference both to her hero Mr Sinatra and to the directness of her lyrics – but with 'Rehab' (which was taken from her second album) she was at her frankest. It was also one of those moments that any artist kills for: a moment that captures everything you'd want in a song. Her chant of 'no, no, no' became ubiquitous across the nation.

Amy is a paid-up subscriber to the school of thought that says if you analyse and discuss your magical talent you might risk losing it. However, she has expanded on how she came to write 'Rehab', and makes the process sound so simple. 'I just sang the hook out loud as a joke. It was quite silly really,' she shrugs. 'I sang the whole line exactly as it turned out on the record! Mark [Ronson] laughed and asked me who wrote it because he liked it. I told him that I'd just made it up but that it was true and he encouraged me to turn it into a song, which took me five minutes. It wasn't hard. It was about what my old management company wanted me to do.'

Can it really be that simple to write a song that combines a wonderfully infectious riff with cheeky lyrics that played into the twenty-first-century obsession with the relationship between celebrity, addiction and rehabilitation? We'd all be doing it if that were so. Perhaps it really is that simple, but only for those who occasionally are struck and blessed by a moment of genius.

Whether or not Amy deserves the title of genius has been the subject of some debate. Those who feel she has not earned such an accolade point to the modern era's overuse of the word and argue that only an innovator can be justly awarded the status of genius and that, given the proudly derivative style of Amy's music, a genius she is not. However, perhaps the entire debate is missing the point. Stand in any bar or club and see the effect that songs like 'Rehab' have on the masses. Watch as everyone in the club mouths along to the 'no, no, no'. Amy's music belongs not just to the intellectuals of the music press whose knowledge of pop history allows them to compare her to acts of yesteryear while rubbing their goatee beards; nor does it belong only to those who foam at the mouth with joy at her latest tabloid discretion. It belongs to all of us. To borrow and adapt a phrase, she is the people's Jewish princess.

Often, artists are merely conduits for a range of human experiences and emotions that they might never have experienced themselves. Witness pop idol Gareth Gates singing 'The Long and Winding Road' at the age of just seventeen. However, in the confessional, touchy-feely twenty-first century, the public is increasingly receptive to artists who bare their souls on stage, singing about their own lives and experiences.

Robbie Williams sang about his own demons in numerous songs including 'Strong' and 'Feel', and Libertines frontmen Pete Doherty and Carl Barat portrayed their intense friendship in 'Can't Stand Me Now'. Concert halls are becoming more like therapy centres with the stage representing the couch and the audience becoming the shrinks. Amy fits as neatly as you like into this atmosphere. Her songs are nakedly about her own experiences. Her first album, *Frank*, was almost entirely about her relationship with one man, and, even when the songs deviated from that theme, their origin was still personal, such as about her father's infidelity.

Her second album, *Back to Black*, was largely about her tumultuous relationship with her husband Blake Fielder-Civil. Again, there were also songs about other aspects of her personal life, including the aforementioned 'Rehab' and also 'Addicted', which is her warning to a flatmate to stop her boyfriend smoking Amy's weed. While Amy's fearlessly honest lyrics may be bad news for those in her life who have their dirty laundry aired over the airwaves, for the public it is a joy to behold an artist who actually is – in that embarrassingly overused phrase – keeping it real. When asked how she would like to be remembered, she replied, 'As genuine.' It's hard to see her wish not being fulfilled, though here's hoping we will not need merely to remember her for a long, long time.

'I'm much harder on myself on the album than I am to any man,' she says of *Frank*. 'I know he couldn't help being a certain way, but it still frustrated me, so I lash out with my lyrics. But I've never had a man come up to me and say, "You hate men don't you?" I love boys. That's my problem. That's why I'm so messed up. My ideal man would not play games. I've met a couple of the most beautiful men in the world, but just because I don't know where their heads are I'm like "You're a headache – goodbye!" I just can't be bothered.'

The honest, confessional nature of her songwriting is no creative accident but is rather a deliberate method and tactic on Amy's part. It is also one that she has learned from her heroes. 'I realised', she once said, 'that the Shangri-Las have pretty much got a song for every stage of a relationship. When you see a boy and you don't even know his name; when you start talking to him; when you start going out with him; and then when you're in love with him; and then when he f**king chucks you – and then you want to kill yourself.'

One can chart those different phases of a relationship through Amy's discography. 'A lot of music now is trying to be cool and, like, "Yeah, I don't really care about you" – a really blasé attitude,' she has said. 'I think it's much nicer to be in love, and throw yourself into it, and want to lie in the road for that person. It's like the difference between having a dance in the middle of the party and standing around the outside with a beer bottle trying to look cool.'

Don't expect Amy to stop reflecting her personal life in her music any time soon. 'If I haven't done it, I just can't put it into a song. It has to be autobiographical.' Songwriting for her is like keeping a journal; it's almost her blog via the airwaves. 'It's an exorcism. I get all my stuff out there. If I didn't have this medium to get my experiences across, I would be lost.'

Returning to those contradictions, where does Amy stand in musical tradition? She has been compared not just to many acts of yesteryear but a lot of today's stars too. This includes male stars and, given their shared passion for drugs, Pete Doherty's name is often mentioned in the same breath as Amy's. The similarities are obvious, and Doherty has been a supportive friend to Amy and her husband Blake.

However, perhaps a more apt comparison would be with Oasis's Noel Gallagher. He and Amy share a remarkable knack for songwriting and a tireless wit, and are both as exciting as interviewees as they are performers. What a breath of fresh air compared with the PR-trained acts who dominate the modern music scene! Also, Gallagher previously took drugs for England, but has since packed them in, without needing rehab to leave them behind. Despite the notoriety she has gained for her ruthless and hedonistic ways, it would be no surprise if tough Amy managed the same transition when the time is right for her.

It's in the arena of interviews where the two are most similar. Indeed, if Amy is open in her lyrics, she is just as honest and frank during her interviews. People speak of 'early disclosers' and Amy is very much on the punctual side: she even once cut her stomach with a shard of broken mirror during one interview. While being quizzed about her self-harming, she was asked how it felt. Her reply was, 'It feels like, "Ow, that fucking hurts." It's probably the worst thing I've done.' Well, it's a succinct answer.

She has described Dido's sound as 'background music – the background to death' and said of pop princess Kylie Minogue, 'she's not an artist... she's a pony.' Elsewhere in interviews she once chimed up with the following sexual confession: 'I would fuck Sting. I don't know about ten hours, though!' In the meantime, she can be just as unpredictable onstage as she is during interviews. As well as the notorious 'you monkey c**ts' incident at the Birmingham National Indoor Arena (NIA) in

2007, she has screamed 'Fuck it, fuck it, fuck it!' into her microphone during a concert in Cornwall, a performance that also featured her hitting her own head with her microphone in frustration at apparently forgetting her lyrics.

As a fan observed, 'The gig became absolutely awful. Members of her entourage were coming on to the stage, obviously worried she couldn't go on, and she would just shout "fuck off" at them. Everyone in the crowd just felt sorry for her.' She has also punched a fan in the face and spat at another during a concert.

However, even though Amy is a self-confessed tomboy – she says she thrived educationally only in classes where there were few boys present for her to muck around with – the most apt comparisons must be made with other female stars. *NME* deputy editor Krissi Murison attempted to place her among the pack. 'Acts like Amy Winehouse and Lily Allen have got opinions falling out everywhere, they don't do what they're supposed to, don't act the way they're supposed to. It's what the world needed.'

Sophie Ellis Bextor took the discussion on a stage when she said, 'When I made my first album, pop was a dirty word. Now you have people like Amy Winehouse and Lily Allen who have helped to make it more popular.'

Natasha Bedingfield echoes this: 'When I started out, if you were blonde you would just do a little pole dance and mime. And I was like, "I want to sing live and write about things that mean something to me." Now it feels like there's a lot more people doing that, and I'm happy about that. Lily and Amy are both very talented. I've just heard Amy Winehouse's album and it's great.'

One music writer was more concise concerning where Amy fits among the modern-day female acts: 'She's like Joss Stone with a bit of mud on her dress.' It was intended as a compliment. Another celebrity fan who appreciated the stand Amy took for her sisters is *Ally McBeal* star Jane Krakowski. 'She can do hip-hop, jazz and soul. She's telling interesting stories from a woman's perspective.' Not that Amy considers herself a women's libber. 'I wouldn't say I'm a feminist, but I don't like girls pretending to be stupid because it's easier.'

As a female artist, Amy has had to contend with being judged disproportionately for the way she looks. With her fluctuating weight and the other by-products of her partying lifestyle, she has at times given the sharp claws of the tabloid press plenty to go at. Her lifestyle, too, seems to be judged disproportionately harshly because she is a woman. When she has missed concerts, or turned up on stage late and the worse for wear, she has received far more censure than, say, Pete Doherty of Babyshambles or Shane MacGowan of the Pogues would. Indeed, those artists' wilder ways seem to have if anything increased their street cred. However, when Amy follows suit she is a 'disgrace' and 'threat to our very way of life'. The miserable *Daily Mail* columnist Amanda Platell is a regular critic of Amy, saying, 'It used to be left to Liam and Noel Gallagher of Oasis to behave badly. Now women are the hooligans. How sad.'

This relentless criticism has led to enormous pain for Amy at times. 'I'm an insecure person,' she says. 'I'm very insecure about the way I look. I mean, I'm a musician, I'm not a model. The more insecure I feel, the more I'd drink.' However, those who have a sense of style are positive about her. Karl Lagerfeld, for instance, is one of the most influential fashion designers on the planet. The slim, snowy-haired friend of the likes of Kate Moss and Kylie Minogue said, 'She's a style icon. She is a beautiful, gifted artist. And I very much like her hairdo. I took it as an inspiration, because, in fact, it was also Brigitte Bardot's hairdo in the late fifties and sixties. And now Amy has made it her own style. So, when I saw her, I knew it was the right moment. Amy is the new Brigitte.'

Victoria Beckham, too, has praised Amy's sense of style and also revealed that she is a fan of her music. 'Amy has a real sense of style that I just love. She's very much a fashion icon and I adore what she wears. She's so unique and original.' She added, 'I've never met her but I just love her music – she's an amazing singer.'

It says much about the wildly differing perceptions there are of Amy that, in the week that Lagerfeld and Beckham spoke out in praise of her style, an American poll voted her the 'dirtiest female celebrity'. She grabbed 47 per cent of the vote. Then, in a survey of 323 men aged sixteen to forty-four by the lads' magazine *Nuts*, she came top of the poll with 48 per cent of the vote as the female celebrity readers would least like to kiss under the mistletoe. Coming second was her new-found admirer Victoria Beckham with 24 per cent of the votes. Then, bizarrely, Amy came third in a poll asking British poker players whom they would least like to come up against during a game of poker.

However, in the really significant poll of that week, Amy was triumphant. Apple's iTunes online music store revealed that *Back to Black* was its bestselling download of 2007. The album *Version* by Mark Ronson – including her rendition of 'Valerie' – came third. Soon after this, *Back to Black* landed the top spot in *Maxim* magazine's end-of-year readers' album poll, beating Radiohead's *In Rainbows* and Kanye West's *Graduation*.

Even those who have thrown insults at Amy, though, are wasting their breath, for she is harder on herself than anyone could be towards her. 'I've also had offers to do modelling and stuff. But I'm, like, "Are they mad?" I'm not exactly an oil painting, am I?' she once said. Again, here are contradictions, for Amy has also said of her appearance, 'I wish my boobies were bigger sometimes, but I like the way I look. I'm both cripplingly stupid and hideous to look at.' She told us once more that she was trouble when she said, 'I'm a bastard, I'm not a nice girl and I'm not an investment.'

Which brings us to Amy's well-documented hedonism. She has admitted to using and becoming addicted to heroin and cocaine. She was once admitted to hospital following an overdose of a spectacular cocktail of drugs. The beautiful musical talent Amy has is all too often cruelly overlooked by those who prefer to concentrate on her wild ways, but her at times destructive lifestyle cannot be ignored, nor that of her husband Blake. Together the pair are fast becoming as notorious as past rock couples such as Michael Hutchence and Paula Yates, Pete Doherty and Kate Moss, and Sid Vicious and Nancy Spungen.

Her parents worry themselves sick as they read the latest headlines about Amy's drug and drink problems. After a particularly lurid story in the papers, her mother sent Amy a text message that read, 'What planet are you on? Call me.' Her father Mitchell worries, too and is tireless in his efforts to protect his daughter. Singer Terra Naomi is a label mate of Amy and was herself once a drug user who had to be taken to rehab by her father. She recalls watching a live performance by Amy, sitting near her family: 'Amy's whole family was there. Amy did put on a good show, but she looked like she was having problems, and seeing her dad have to watch that... It was just sad, really sad.'

Amy, however, remains honest about her lifestyle. She shrugs off the notion that working in the music industry means 'there's just so much opportunity to go out every night and get smashed'. Once asked to describe the mission statement behind her songwriting, she said she wrote, 'Songs that you can sing into a bottle of whisky.'

For every moralistic tabloid critic that Amy's attitude throws up, it also attracts her new fans. Celebrated columnist Julie Burchill says, 'I like Amy Winehouse – she's my new favourite. She's a tough old bird and she's not a cry-baby. And she's absolutely beautiful. Amy Winehouse is like a pocket Venus.' As we'll see, Winehouse's and Burchill's paths once crossed in a somewhat surreal fashion.

Burchill's admiration of Winehouse proves that not everyone has been grasped by this bizarre wish to see musical artists become puritanical, milk-guzzling, jogging, health freaks. Somewhere in recent times many people changed from wanting our pop and rock idols to be the wild children who lived the lifestyle we all dream of to wanting them to become 'a good example' (copyright *Daily Mail*). Just as Burchill sees through this nonsense, so does producer Mark Ronson: 'Amy is bringing a rebellious rock'n'roll spirit back to popular music,' he says. 'Those girls from the sixties like the Shangri-Las had that kind of attitude: young girls from Queens in motorcycle jackets.'

It seems ludicrous, but once again it is worth reiterating: Amy Winehouse is a hugely gifted and talented musician. Put aside the controversy and just give her CDs a spin. You'll luxuriate in the warmth and sheer emotion of her voice, the clever, open and honest lyrics. The same goes for her live performances. Of late, there have been so many headlines about her no-shows or drunken shows that, were an alien to be reading the press, he or she would be hard pushed to believe that thousands and thousands have been taken to almost religious levels of joy. It's a joy shared by Amy, who says, 'Basically, I live to do gigs... it's my life.'

Given the rich maturity of her voice, and the success she has already enjoyed, it is easy to forget how young Amy still is. She has not, at the time of writing, yet reached that dangerous rock-and-roll age of twenty-seven. It was at this age that Janis Joplin, Doors singer Jim Morrison, Jimi Hendrix and Kurt Cobain all died, at the height of their infamy. There's no disputing that she has issues with drugs to overcome, but the longer her true story goes on, the more clear it seems that Amy will neither burn out nor fade away but instead go on to even greater (natural) highs.

This book might surprise those who like to see Amy as 'out of control' or 'spiralling towards death', to use two of the tabloid press's favourite phrases when discussing her life. Getting to the truth behind the hype, it instead paints a portrait of an intensely shrewd, witty and grounded woman. She knows how to play the tortured soul for the press, because she knows that is the Amy they wish to portray. Always one to play the press at their own game, when she once knew there was a press pack waiting outside a club for her, she painted a false tear on her cheek and rubbed quite innocent white powder all over her nostrils. Some of the papers got the joke the next day, but it went right over the heads of others and they painted it not as a joke by Amy but as a *real* tear and *real* cocaine.

So let's ride the roller coaster that is Amy Winehouse's life, from the hit records and prestigious awards to the overdoses and scraps with husband Blake. While riding these ups and downs, we'll uncover the *real* Amy Winehouse – an act who does indeed have a glittering future, but also a fascinating past.

Chapter One

BORN TO BE WILD?

It was once said of Amy Winehouse, 'She often strikes as a personality born slightly out of time.' She was born on 14 September 1983, in Southgate, north London. Less than ten miles from central London and within the borough of Enfield, Southgate is adjacent to the North Circular Road. Other famous – and not so famous – people to have been born in Southgate over the years include Conservative Party legend Norman Tebbit and S Club 7 singer Rachel Stevens.

Many of the families who live within the redbrick houses of Southgate are Jewish. Jewish people have lived in the Enfield area since 1750 but it was between World Wars One and Two that many Jewish families moved from east to north London. By the time of the Swinging Sixties, around 280,000 Jews were living in north London. There are now five synagogues and three Jewish cemeteries within easy reach of Southgate.

Although there are photographs of Amy dressed up in costume for the Jewish festival of Purim, hers was not an especially religious family. 'We didn't grow up religious. I'm just a real family girl. I come from a big family. I think it's important to have your family around you, to be close to your family. I'm very lucky I have a mum and dad.'

Zeddy Lawrence, editor of *Jewish News*, says, 'She's been happy to talk about her Jewish identity. I don't know that she's milked her Jewishness that much, to be honest. She's not ashamed of mentioning that she's Jewish or talking about that, but there are very few interviews where the Jewish thing has come out.

'As far as the Jewish community goes, I think we were very excited when she first came on the scene. We wondered who this Jewish pop star was. There are very few of them about apart from Rachel Stevens, who didn't have much credibility because she was in S Club 7. Stevens was just good-looking with a nice pair of breasts, if you'll excuse me for saying that. She has talent, I suppose, but she was very much a pop princess.

'But in terms of a Jewish artist, I think it had been a long time since there was anyone like that. I can't remember the last credible Jewish artist in England. Amy came across as a credible artist, so there was a lot of excitement in the community because of that. I think since then she's fallen out of favour a lot because of her behaviour.'

Amy says she didn't enjoy going to *cheder* classes – the

traditional elementary school teaching the basics of Judaism and the Hebrew language. 'Every week I'd say "I don't want to go, Dad, please don't make me go," she says. 'He was so soppy he often let me off. I never learnt anything about being Jewish when I went anyway.' However, she does attend synagogue on Yom Kippur and observes the Passover festival. 'Being Jewish to me is about being together as a real family,' she concludes. 'It's not about lighting candles and saying a *brocha*.

'I'm not religious at all. I think faith is something that gives you strength. I believe in fate and I believe that things happen for a reason but I don't think that there's a high power, necessarily. I believe in karma very much, though. There are so many rude people around and they're the people that don't have any real friends. And relationships with people – with your mum, your nan, your dog – are what you get the most happiness in life from. Apart from shoes and bags.'

Family girl Amy was brought up in a neat, detached home by her parents Mitchell and Janis. Mitchell Winehouse, known as Mitch, was a taxi driver and amateur singer. He was a big fan of artists such as Tony Bennett and Frank Sinatra and the sounds of these men's music filled the house as Amy grew up. 'My dad's great,' says Amy. 'He's like the karaoke Sinatra. He has a CD in his cab of all the backing tracks. He could be a lounge act, he's that good.'

Mitch's mother, too, had links with music. She had once dated the legendary musician and jazz club owner Ronnie Scott. However, the relationship hit an impenetrable Catch 22. 'She wouldn't have sex with him until they married, and he wanted to marry her but wouldn't unless they had sex before 'cos he didn't know whether he would enjoy himself. So he went off.'

Mitchell, in defending his daughter, once said, 'My daughter isn't drug-crazed. Even when I was a young man I dabbled – what young person hasn't?' He adds, 'What Amy writes is true to life, and sometimes it's painful. "What Is It About Men?" was fair enough. She didn't lie about it – she wrote, "All the shit my mother went through." It was true. I did put her mother through a lot of shit. But I was only unfaithful to her once.'

However, she is keen to stress that she received lots of love and affection from her father. 'When I was little, if I walked into a room where my dad was, I'd get kissed and cuddled by him. He was the same with my mum when they were still together. Because he was so like that, she was less so.' She has also said that she is 'a lot like my dad. We're both the sort of characters who believe it's important to get stuff done and to be honest with people.'

Mitchell remembers singing along with Amy when she was a child. He would begin singing a song – Frank Sinatra's 'I Only Have Eyes for You', for instance – and then leave occasional lines out, allowing Amy to fill the gaps. 'Mitchell and Amy were close,' remembers her mother Janis. 'Her father would sing Sinatra to her and, because he always sang, she was always singing, even in school. Her teachers had to tell her to stop doing it in lessons.' Janis, who took an Open University science degree before studying at the London School of Pharmacy, also had musical connections: her brothers were professional jazz musicians. The couple had moved from a cramped two-bedroom flat to a thirties semi to a pretty three-bedroom Victorian terrace in Southgate.

There they had their first child, Alex, and then, four years later, Amy. 'Amy was a beautiful child – always busy, always curious,' remembers Janis. Scare stories about Amy's chaotic lifestyle now regularly fill the newspapers and as a child she had two memorable brushes with disaster: as a toddler she nearly choked on Cellophane while sitting in her pram, and she once went missing in the local park. One of Amy's early memories is having a crush on the children's television presenter Philip Schofield. She used to urge her mother to leave her father and marry Schofield instead.

Amy also enjoyed being with her grandmother, who introduced Amy and her brother to grooming. 'God rest her soul, she pretty much trained me and my brother. He'd give her a pedicure and I'd do her nails and her hair,' said Amy. On hearing this, her husband Blake joked, 'It might be quite emasculating for a young boy of eight to be pedicuring his grandmother.'

Her nan was clearly a big influence on Amy. When asked about her phobias, she said, 'I don't think I'm scared of anything. I'm not scared of snakes or spiders or anything. But I am scared of my nan. She's little, but she's a frightening person.' Not that after-school television and beauty training from her nan were Amy's only joys. 'I really liked school, I liked learning,' she recalls, adding, 'but I suppose if you don't feel like an outsider, you never do anything out of the box, do you? So I must have felt like an outsider a bit. But it's not a sob story.'

Asked whether they can cite any childhood influences on Amy, Mitchell points to Janis. 'The influence comes from my ex-wife's family... there are some excellent musicians in there. But it's more what we listened to at home: Sinatra, Ella Fitzgerald, Dinah Washington.' As for Janis, she passes the credit back to Mitchell. 'Like any parent with talented children I'm hugely proud of their achievements but can honestly say I've never pushed or cajoled them into show business. I just want them to be happy. I'm not in awe of greatness and don't take special credit for the way their talents have risen to the surface.'

Janis confirms, 'It's always been her dream to be a singer. That was all she ever wanted. She was always singing around the house.' She would sing 'I Will Survive' by Gloria Gaynor while lying in the bath. Neighbours, too, remember the early Amy Winehouse performances – and her fledgling cheek! Paul Nesbitt lived near the Winehouse family. He said, 'When I moved in, Amy popped her head out of her bedroom window and started singing with a microphone. She was talented. But she was a bit naughty. There was a bald copper who lived opposite and Amy would shout "slaphead" at him. She'd hold parties when her mum had gone out.'

Her brother Alex, too, was a huge music fan and therefore a big influence on Amy's development in the field. She says, 'As a little kid I was too shy to sing and my brother was the one standing on a chair in his school uniform and doing his Frank Sinatra.' His ability on the guitar inspired Amy to learn. 'He taught himself, so I took inspiration for teaching myself from him and he showed me a couple of things,' she has said. 'He was into jazz music when he was eighteen and I was fourteen and I'd hear Thelonious Monk, Dinah Washington, Sarah Vaughn and Ella Fitzgerald; and I learnt to sing by listening,' she says.

Her first guitar was a Fender Stratocaster 'It's my favourite guitar,' she said many years later. 'It's classic, it looks good and it sounds beautiful. It really lends itself to anything.' However, she has also awarded the 'favourite guitar' tag to another model. 'The Gretch White Falcon is my favourite guitar of all time. It's beautiful. There's this great picture of a falcon on the scratch plate.'

Young Amy was eventually to step out of Alex's musical shadow. 'When I was about nine, I did it,' she recalls. '"Sing!" my nana would shout. "And smile!" But I still needed to hold a fan to my face for "Eternal Flame": "Close your eyes, give me your hand..."'

Amy's best friend is Juliette Ashby. As children the pair would play a game. 'She was Pepsi and I was Shirley, the backing girls for Wham!. I think we clicked because we were both a bit off-key.' This soon led the pair to form their own double-act called Sweet 'n' Sour. 'Me and my friend loved Salt-N-Pepa,' she explains. 'So we formed a band called Sweet 'n' Sour. We had a tune called "Spinderella", which was great... but it was a long time ago.'

Salt-N-Pepa were more than mere pop stars to the young Amy. 'My first real role models were Salt-N-Pepa,' she says. 'They were real women who weren't afraid to talk about men, and they got what they wanted and talked about girls they didn't like. That was always really cool.'

More traditional pop girls had held little appeal for Amy. 'I liked forward-thinking hip-hop like Mos Def, and conscious stuff like Nas,' she said. 'You know how there's always one artist who makes you realise what it means to be an artist? I was into Kylie Minogue and Madonna, and then I discovered Salt-N-Pepa, and I realised there are real women making music.' As well as 'Spinderella', Sweet 'n' Sour's other song titles included 'Who Are the Glam Chicks (Us)?' and 'Boys (Who Needs Them?)', the latter of which was a precocious sign of themes to come.

Amy recalls, 'There was jazz but hip-hop was running through me, too. When I was nine or ten, me and my friends all loved En Vogue.' However it was at the age of thirteen that one of Amy's key musical moments occurred. One day she heard 'Leader of the Pack', by the Shangri-Las and fell in love with the girl band's sound. More than anything, this moment pushed her towards a career in music herself. One of America's leading girl groups of the 1960s, the Shangri-Las performed songs that were concerned with lost love and other teenage dramas. As well as 'Leader of the Pack', their other well-known songs include 'Remember (Walking in the Sand)' (later covered by rockers Aerosmith), 'Out in the Streets' (covered by Blondie), and the war romance classic 'Long Live Our Love'.

As well as the sounds of jazz music filling the house, visitors were always coming and going and it was a happy household for Amy initially. Her schooldays were filled with fun, and it was at the age of four that Amy first met her friend Juliette Ashby at Osidge Primary School. The school's website nowadays has a mini-manifesto on its homepage. Among its policies are 'We recognise that children are individuals and have different needs.' Well, Amy and Juliette were definitely individuals from the start. They would egg each other on to do naughty things. 'We were a bit nutty,' recalls Ashby, 'and we were always in trouble.' They would therefore often find themselves at the school reception desk, where pupils were sent if they had misbehaved. One day, as they stood at the desk, they told a male pupil that if he didn't pull his pants down that they would no longer remain friends with him. The schoolboy duly obliged and Ashby recalls that incident as the one that made them truly bond. The friendship remains strong to this day but there were difficult moments back in the school days. Ashby claims she once made Amy a friendship brooch but that her friend ungratefully threw it in a sandpit.

'She's an idiot – I never did that,' counters Amy. 'She was the one with the upper hand. Juliette always had strawberry shoelaces in her bag, and you knew you were flavour of the day if she offered you one.' Ashby admits that their friendship has at times been tested. 'Like when she acts like a dickhead and I have to pick her up, which is more or less all the time.'

Even so, Ashby utterly trusts her friend. 'We both know that we'd rescue each other from a burning building if we had to. We've got that understanding. You can rely on your friends to be there when your family have totally washed their hands of you.'

One of their favourite tricks involved one of the pair running from the classroom in floods of tears, whereupon the other would say that they'd have to go out and comfort her. 'And then we'd just sit in a room somewhere, laughing for the rest of the lesson,' says Ashby. Little surprise, then, that teachers would try to split the pair up. Indeed, once they progressed to secondary school, even the girls' mothers pleaded with the school to not let their girls sit together. Consequently, they hardly saw each other between the ages of thirteen and fifteen. 'I was a proper little shit,' admits Amy. 'I used to bunk off school and get my boyfriend round. My mum used to come home from work at lunchtime and we'd be lying around in dressing gowns!

'I was cute up to the age of about five but then I got naughty. I was very naughty. Very, very, very naughty. When everyone else went out for first play we went through all their lunchboxes and ate all their crisps. And, when they came in from play, half of their lunches would be missing. I grew out of it by the time I was about nine, though.'

When Janis wrote an open letter to her daughter through the pages of the *News of the World* in 2007, she spoke of Amy's childhood:

> Even when you were only a rosy-cheeked five-year-old singing into a hairbrush in front of the mirror, you had a will as stubborn as a mule. Do you remember? We couldn't ever get you to see things from any angle other than your own. You could swear day was night and Heaven help anyone who tried to disagree.
>
> You were never a wayward daughter but you always had a strong will and a mind of your own – qualities your father and I were so proud of. You were well brought up, you had a keen sense of right from wrong and you

understood the values we always impressed on you as a family. But you would never be pressurised or influenced into doing something if your heart wasn't in it.

Do you remember those Decembers long ago when I used to swaddle you in a thick winter coat? I used to wrap you up and give you a kiss on the nose before you went out to play in the cold. 'Don't worry about me Ma, I'll be fine!' you used to laugh. But, like any mother, of course I worried.

Amy's naughtiness came from boredom at school. She felt smothered and frustrated by the regimen of education. 'I didn't like being told what to do,' she shrugs, the scowl returning to her face. 'I was on report all the time. It gets to you after a while, having to sign a piece of paper after every lesson. So I left.'

By this time, Amy had endured the painful experience of watching her parents split up. 'We never argued,' Janis remembers of the circumstances leading to the split. 'We'd had a very agreeable marriage but he was never there. He was… away a lot, but for a long time there was also another woman, Jane, who became his second wife. I think Mitchell would have liked to have both of us but I wasn't happy to do that.'

For any child of nine, to watch their parents split up would be almost unbearably difficult. For Amy, the experience was typically painful and her mother believes that this has influenced Amy's music. 'People talk a lot about the anger in Amy's songs,' said Janis. 'I think a lot of it was that her father wasn't there. Now he's trying to make up for that and he's spending more time with her, but what he's doing now is what he should have been doing then.'

Interestingly, a live performance at Shepherds Bush Empire once saw Amy spend a lot of time during the show gazing up at Blake, who was in the circle to the right of the stage. As she sang lines about his infidelities, she fixed her focus on him. However, she also spun round and sang a few of the lines at her father Mitch, who was in the circle to the left of the stage. Nowadays, Amy sniffs, 'My dad was shady. He moved house every two years – I've no idea what he was running from.'

An old 'friend' of Amy's spoke about this period of her life in an interview with a celebrity magazine. 'After Amy's dad Mitch moved out when she was nine, she felt that she could do anything she wanted,' reveals the old pal. 'She started wearing short skirts and makeup. Her mum Janis struggled to control her. Amy lost her virginity at fifteen... and told her mum, who made her go on the Pill. She was treated badly by the boy and I don't think her head was in a good space about it. It traumatised her and she speaks about it even now.'

Recently, Amy returned to her first school and the visit turned out to be suitably chaotic. 'My old teacher was there – this cold-blooded bitch, she bleeds ice. She's had the same haircut since 1840,' chuckles Amy. 'I was there with my friend and after the shoot we were like, "Miss, hello, miss, can we have a look round the school?" She was like, grudgingly, "OK", and we went to the art room and my friend wandered off. Next thing, he shouted, "Run! I've smashed the fire alarm!" and the whole school was evacuated. It was the highlight of my life. I was saying, "I do hope it's just a drill, miss" – and her face was a picture.'

As a child Amy was comforted not only by her love of music: she was also a huge fan of American wrestling. An unnamed friend recalls that she was addicted to shows such as *SmackDown* and *Raw*. She even got to meet one of her heroes, Chris Jericho, who was one of the biggest names in the sport. 'Amy was so excited about meeting him, she wouldn't stop talking about it. She was much more excited to meet a wrestler than any musician.' She was also a fan of Rob Van Dam and would, reportedly, 'go crazy' whenever he was on TV.

At the age of twelve, Amy took the first step towards fame herself.

Chapter Two

DRAMA QUEEN

The Sylvia Young Theatre School was originally established in 1981 on Drury Lane. It moved to Marylebone in 1983. Such has been the success of the school that Young herself was given an OBE in 2005. However, it has also been the subject of controversy, with actress Billie Piper claiming in her autobiography that students were encouraged to become 'lighter, smaller and thinner' and that eating disorders among the students were often ignored by teachers.

Fellow Sylvia Young graduate Denise Van Outen was outraged by Piper's comments. She stormed, 'I was a big Billie Piper fan, but in her book she was very negative about Sylvia and the school and I think that's wrong and unfair. If it wasn't for Sylvia, she wouldn't be where she is. And she really wouldn't be where she is because she got all her breaks during her schooling years.' Young herself was more to the point, describing Piper's remarks as 'poisonous'.

Sylvia Young remembers Amy very well. 'It is hard to overstate just how much she struck me as unique, both as a composer and performer, from the moment she first came through the doors at the age of thirteen, sporting the same distinctive hairstyle that she has now,' she says, adding that she believes Amy could well have become like Judy Garland or Ella Fitzgerald. 'But the emphasis is on that word "could". Sadly, there is a danger that Amy will be better known for her personal life than for her God-given musical gifts.'

Young remembers her first encounter with Amy. 'She was one of a crowd of enthusiastic new pupils milling around the old-fashioned corridors of our school. I auditioned her myself. She did some acting, and showed great potential. She danced for us and proved she was a good mover. When she sang, however, we were blown away. It was not quite such a deep voice as she has now, of course. But her delivery of "On the Sunny Side of the Street" was rich and wonderful all the same.' Amy was offered a scholarship and Young says that she very quickly realised she had not just a huge talent on her hands, but also a 'real character' who was in her own world and insisted on doing things her own way. Like all applicants, Amy was asked to write a short essay, explaining why she wanted to come to the school.

This is what she wrote:

All my life I have been loud, to the point of being told to

shut up. The only reason I have had to be this loud is because you have to scream to be heard in my family.

My family? Yes, you read it right. My Mum's side is perfectly fine, my Dad's family are the singing, dancing, all-nutty musical extravaganza.

I've been told I was gifted with a lovely voice and I guess my Dad's to blame for that.

Although unlike my Dad, and his background and ancestors, I want to do something with the talents I've been 'blessed' with.

My Dad is content to sing loudly in his office and sell windows. My mother, however, is a chemist. She is quiet, reserved.

I would say that my school life and school reports are filled with 'could do betters' and 'does not work to her full potential'.

I want to go somewhere where I am stretched right to my limits and perhaps even beyond.

To sing in lessons without being told to shut up (provided they are singing lessons).

But mostly I have this dream to be very famous. To work on stage. It's a lifelong ambition.

I want people to hear my voice and just... forget their troubles for five minutes.

I want to be remembered for being an actress, a singer, for sellout concerts and sellout West End and Broadway shows.

For being just... me.

The first half of Amy's first week at the school was spent doing standard academic studies, and then in the second half she studied dance. 'She was completely focused on her music, showing dedication and high standards,' Sylvia Young remembers. 'But nothing else interested her and, when she wasn't singing, she was naughty. The misdemeanours were never serious, but they were persistent.'

The misdemeanours included not wearing her school uniform in the correct manner, chewing gum during class and wearing a silver nose ring. Young asked Amy to remove it which she did – only to replace it an hour later. 'We found a way of coexisting,' Amy's teacher remembers. 'She would break the rules; I would tell her off; and she would acknowledge it. She could be disruptive in class, too, but this was largely because she didn't concentrate.'

Amy was also not overfriendly with her fellow pupils. 'I wasn't gregarious,' she shrugs. There were lots of totally insufferable kids there who'd come into class and announce, "My mummy's coming to pick me up for an audition at three o'clock." I was a little weirdo, I suppose, in that young, random way, but I wasn't a loner. Friends would go, "Come and be weird with us!"'

Amy was, however, in Young's own words 'wonderfully clever'. She particularly enjoyed English lessons. She was, accordingly, moved one year ahead of her age group. 'In class she would write extraordinary notes to her friends. These were not mere jottings. Amy was prolific. Every millimetre of the page was crammed with her writing, which seemed to flow off the paper with her energy.' These notes would frequently include swearwords and sometimes lyrics, too.

Amy says now, 'I was at stage school for a year and a half but all I did was sing songs with other people. You can't be taught how to sing. After I left school I wanted to earn a living and I got lucky when a friend of a friend came to see me at a jazz gig and helped me get a break.'

One of her fellow pupils was Matt Willis, who went on to find fame with the pop band Busted and then as the king of the jungle on *I'm a Celebrity, Get Me Out of Here!*. 'We all loved Matt at school and, yeah, I fancied him. I still do, he's a lovely boy.' Busted's label mates and friends McFly are led by singer/songwriter Tom Fletcher, who remembers Amy from Sylvia Young, too. 'I think she was asked to leave, which is the polite way of saying she was expelled,' he says. 'She was always in trouble, as far as I remember. I didn't really know her but I saw her at school every day. She liked to speak her mind. I don't remember ever hearing her sing.'

As we'll see, the expulsion rumour was a misunderstanding.

Gem Allen, a fellow pupil, says there were few signs of Amy's future wild ways back at Sylvia Young Theatre School. 'I wouldn't have predicted she would go as wild as this. Some pictures of her now are heartbreaking. I just think, "She's my old schoolfriend, I hope she's OK." I hope Amy's sorting herself out but it is shocking to see things such as when she pulled out of the MTV awards. I couldn't believe it because that had always been her dream.

'Amy was a character at school. She was a wild girl but it was different from the trouble she's in now. She would call herself a witch. She used to joke she could put spells on people. One time she lay on the floor in the history class and started crawling along towards Billie, saying, "Wilhelmina" – her nickname for Billie – "I'm coming to get you" in a witchy voice.'

Naughty as Amy could be at times, reports that she was expelled from the school are dismissed as a 'myth' by Young. She claims that, without her knowledge, another teacher rang Amy's mother and told her she would fail her GCSEs unless she was removed from the school. Young was livid. 'I was very unhappy to discover this, and the teacher who made the call left us shortly afterwards,' she snaps. 'I told Amy's mother that she wasn't the type of child who naturally enjoys a school environment but that she would be happier with us and the vocational side of her studies than in an all-girl academic school.'

Janis remembers, 'The principal phoned up and asked me to come in and see him. He said, "I think you should take her away." He didn't want children who weren't going to get good grades and Amy wasn't going to. She was very bright but she was always messing around. The same day, I had to take the family cat Katie to the vet. I dropped off the cat, went to the school and then went back to the vet's. We had the cat put down. My joke is I should have had Amy put down and the cat moved on.'

So it was that Amy was removed from the school. She says that she 'cried every night' after she left. 'The thing about stage school is that it prepares you as a person,' she has said since. 'It's excellent for building character.' So impressed was Young with her former student that she stayed in touch with her.

'When I left Sylvia Young, I hated school so much that I didn't want to go at all. That was horrid. I was gutted when I left, because there are some really dedicated people there, and Sylvia herself is brilliant. I pierced my nose when I was thirteen. They didn't like that. I brought my guitar to school every day because I was a guitarist and they'd tell me I couldn't. I was like, "Well, look, I'm a singer, a musician, not an academic..." But that's what made me a better person, it showed me that you can't really be taught stuff: you have to go out there and find out for yourself.

She then attended the Mount School in Mill Hill. Established in May 1925, the Mount has as its motto 'To be, rather than to seem to be'. When it was last inspected, the report found that it had a friendly, family atmosphere, with a caring and supportive ethos. Amy, though, was bored out of her wits there.

'There was nothing to do at that school but run the teachers,' she says, referring to the absence of the opposite gender to taunt and tease. 'I got a D in music because my teacher wouldn't submit my course work because I used to be so nasty.'

Cannabis was a great comfort to her at this point, as was music of course. Her favourite around this time included Charlie Mingus, Thelonious Monk, Dinah Washington, Clifford Brown and Sarah Vaughan. 'To hear subtle music like that, like a trio could give more to me than a big band, that's when I learned about less is more,' she said. 'I started loving jazz and getting so much from it. There was nothing out there for me [musically]. Everything I liked, to this day, that was new was spoken word, rappers. To me that's the new jazz. I'm talking about progressive rap, not stuff like P Diddy. Mos Def, Nas, Busta Rhymes – those are the Miles [Davis] to me now.'

Even at this point, Amy's relatives were already doing their best to drum up support for her musical career. Iconic writer Julie Burchill is, as we've seen, an enthusiastic admirer of Amy nowadays. However, in an interview with the author, Burchill reveals that she was first made aware of Amy years before she became famous. While Burchill was making a television programme about her father's death from asbestosis, she crossed paths with Amy's aunt, Debra Milne, who is a consultant histopathologist in Sunderland. Milne examined Burchill's father's autopsy for the programme and is featured talking to her on camera.

'When the cameras stopped rolling,' remembers Burchill, 'she asked me, "Do you still write about music?" I said, "Not really," and Debra added, "Because I wondered if you'd like to see my niece next week. She's really great though she's only sixteen. Her name is Amy Winehouse. Years later, suddenly Amy was everywhere I looked. Names are the one thing I always remember, and also because it was a Jewish name and so pretty it stuck in my mind particularly.'

Around the same time, Amy had her first, fleeting, brush with fame when she appeared on the BBC comedy sketch programme *The Fast Show*. Created by university pals Charlie Higson and Paul Whitehouse, *The Fast Show* was a hit throughout for the 1990s with its characters such as Ted and Ralph, and the Suits You duo. Another memorable character was Competitive Dad, and it was in one of his sketches that

Amy bursts onto the scene with a series of live performances…

Above left: At the Shepherds Bush Empire in November 2003.

Above right: A shy-looking Amy before performing at a Virgin Megastore in London in December 2003.

Below left: A month later, here she is wowing the crowds at HMV Oxford Street, January 2004.

Below right: Performing at the Nominations show for the 2004 BRIT Awards.

A voluptuous Amy at the 2004 Mercury Music Prize, where her debut record *Frank* was shortlisted for the Album of the Year.

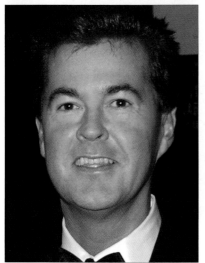

Above left: Amy's mum Janis.

Above right: Sylvia Young, of the Sylvia Young Theatre School where Amy trained from 12 to 14. She was unruly but loved.

Below left: Simon Fuller, pop mogul and owner of 19 Management and its subsidiary Brilliant 19, who managed Amy in the early days of her career.

Below right: The BRIT School, Croydon, another former *alma mater* of Amy's.

Above left: May 2004, and Amy poses with her award for Best Contemporary Song at the 49th annual Ivor Novello Awards, given for her song 'Stronger than Me'. She was to win another Ivor Novello three years later for her song 'Rehab'.

Above right: Amy performs songs from her first album *Frank* at the V Festival in Chelmsford, August 2004.

Below: December 31st 2006, and Jools Holland and friends see in the New Year in style on BBC TV with his 'Hootenanny' musical spectacular. Amy made the party go with a swing as she belted out a cover of Marvin Gaye's 'I Heard It Through the Grapevine', accompanied by legendary singer-songwriter Paul Weller.

Above left: Amy wins Pop awards at South Bank Show, 23 January 2007.

Above right: Valentine's Day 2007, and it's the BRIT Awards. A sultry-looking Amy performs on stage at Earl's Court. Her album *Back to Black* was nominated for best album, but honours came her way for Best British Female Solo Artist instead.

Below left: Sitting pretty… Amy records a special for the BBC in March 2007.

Below right: MTV Live, Toronto, Canada, May 2007. Before an intimate audience of fans, Amy takes part in her first in-studio interview for the music channel.

Above left: Amy and her husband Blake Fielder-Civil attend the 2007 MTV Movie Awards at Universal City Walk, Los Angeles, USA in June. 'Rehab' peaked at Number 9 on the Billboard Hot 100 a week after it was performed at the awards show.

Above right: Amy on Parkie. Back fresh from LA, and flavour of the moment everywhere, Amy appears on the long-running British chat show *Parkinson*.

Below: A slightly nervous Amy performs on the Pyramid Stage in front of huge crowds on the first day of the 2007 Glastonbury Festival.

Amy at one of her favourite local watering holes, The Hawley Arms, Camden – a Mecca for starspotters and trend-followers.

Amy in classic pose.

Amy appeared. Dressed as a fairy in a school production of *A Midsummer Night's Dream*, Amy acts with other children onstage until an exasperated Competitive Dad heckles and goes up on stage himself. In 2007, Paul Whitehouse revealed that the young girl on the stage was Amy. 'We didn't know she was going to be famous at the time,' he said. 'We only found out about it when she mentioned it in an interview.' The *Daily Mail* duly made the link public, headlining its story, AMY WINEHOUSE ON TV BEFORE SHE WAS INFAMOUS.

However, perhaps the most significant outcome from the Sylvia Young school for Amy came in the form of the friendship she found there with a young man from Canning Town, south London, called Tyler James. James grew up in a household dominated by women after his dad left home, and his childhood home was always full of music with his mother's recordings of Motown acts such as Stevie Wonder, the Supremes, Marvin Gaye and Bob Marley. His elder sister added TLC, SWV and Erykah Badu. As for James himself, he was a fan of Babyface, Boyz II Men and mainstream jazz acts. He went on to become a soul singer of some repute, winning the T4 One To Watch award at the *Smash Hits* Poll Winners Party in 2005. He said, 'In ten years' time I want to be able to look at myself and say "Yeah, I started off with few opportunities in life and look where I am now." I want that feeling of satisfaction; I want to make my mum proud; I want to make my family proud and I think I can do that and make a record that I'm proud of.'

His debut album, *The Unlikely Lad* – which included a duet

with Amy on the track 'Best of Me' – received praise from many. *The Sun* described him as the UK's answer to Justin Timberlake – praise indeed. 'A refreshingly modern album drawing on vintage soul, jazz and pop,' gushed the *Observer*, adding that it was 'likeable and human'.

The Times declared,

Despite sporting the worst haircut since that bloke from *A Flock of Seagulls*, James demonstrates, on his new single, 'Foolish', that he can cut the mustard (the retro, big-band video is superb) and carry a tune... With radio support, James will be mega, dodgy thatch or not.

The *Daily Star* described him as 'less gobby' than Amy. 'His music is a slick mix of funky rhythms and cool-as-ice vocals. He was also praised by *NME*, *Time Out* and *Face*.'

Amy described herself and James as 'mates who shag... My Nan thinks he looks like Leonardo DiCaprio but he's much better-looking.'

They took it in turns to do the washing-up. 'If I've been in all day, I'll have his dinner ready when he comes home. I do everything for him, but we have our own lives. I'm a very sexual person but sex is a minor thing in our relationship – we've got so much more than that. And we let each other see other people. Tyler might stay away for a couple of days with a girl. We don't just sit around and cuddle like your average couple: we give each other space.' However, James was soon to give Amy something far more significant than space.

A spell at the BRIT Performing Arts & Technology School in Croydon followed for Amy. The school, which has been compared to New York High School for the Performing Arts – the subject of 1980s film *Fame* – is funded by the Department for Innovation, Universities and Skills, but independent of the local education authority's control. Since 1992 it has received sponsorship from the BRIT Trust, the body behind the BRIT Awards, where Amy was to achieve recognition further down the line. It has a fantastic academic record: in 2006 for instance, 93 per cent of its pupils gained five or more 'A' to 'C' grades in GCSEs.

(Incidentally, the first fully selective arts academy is now being built in Birmingham. Based on the BRIT School, the Birmingham institution in the city's Eastside will train students in music, theatre, painting and other arts. The school, which will teach up to 950 pupils aged fourteen to nineteen, is one of three academies planned in the city.)

Among those who have studied at the BRIT are the Kooks, Katie Melua, Floetry, Dane Bowers, the Feeling, the Noisettes, Imogen Heap and Leona Lewis. One teacher observed that the BRIT school is for 'the non-type. The school fits round their personality, rather than asking them to fit their personality round the school.' Another adds that many of their pupils might have had negative experiences in their past, due to their creativity – 'like bullying or being the only boy dancer in a south London comprehensive – before they came here'.

It has been said that the best way to find the school is 'to take a train from London Bridge, disembark at Selhurst and follow the teen wearing bright-yellow drainpipe jeans, a leather motorcycle jacket and bird's-nest hairstyle'. There's a lot of truth to it. When Amy first arrived at the school she found two main buildings: an oblong pavilion and redbrick building, which was built in 1907. There are at any given time 850 pupils studying at the school, all of whom enrol at the age of fourteen or sixteen. As a state-funded creative school, it is very popular and only one in three applicants is successful, as Amy was.

One teacher remembers Amy as being 'exciting, but nerve-racking. She was an artist from the age of sixteen, and she wasn't exactly suited to being institutionalised.' Nick Williams, the principal, agrees: 'You would have had to be mad not to realise that Amy was a very, very talented young woman and that she had what it took to be extremely successful. Katie Melua and Amy Winehouse are two very different people – the one thing they have in common is that there isn't anyone who is exactly like them. They're not factory-farmed. What we do is attract people into the school who are creative – that means things will happen.

'We acknowledge that when kids leave here and find their way their experiences might be harsher, edgier or more difficult. We see no purpose in treating young people in a competitive way. Lots of bands don't want to talk about coming from the BRIT School, and the reason is obvious: if you're in a band, you don't want people to feel that, somehow, someone allowed you to do that. I'm really sanguine about people who leave the school and say, "I did this, it's nothing to do with where I went to school." '

As for Amy, the advantage of the BRIT school was that there were hardly any boys. 'I was like, "Where's the men? What is going on?" So I used to lock myself away from the time of fifteen and just do music, because I hated the school. Every lunchtime, every break, I'd be up in the music room playing a guitar or piano.'

As well as her hours in the music room, it was this time that Amy first fell in love with getting tattoos. 'I just wanted a Betty Boop on my bum,' she chuckled. 'I just like tattoos. My parents pretty much realised that I would do whatever I wanted, and that was it, really.'

Of her experiences of two stage schools, Amy is as forthright as one would expect. 'I'm always happy to blow up any misconceptions that people have about stage school 'cos everyone thinks it's really nasty there, but it's not,' she says of the star-maker factory. 'I went to the BRIT School as well and that was shit. But Sylvia Young set me up to be a strong person,' she decides. So it's not all boobs out, bums in? 'No, it is like that, but...'

Amy might be dismissive of the BRIT School but many associated with it are hugely proud of her involvement. BBC 6 Music DJ Natasha Desborough said, 'The likes of the Kooks and Amy Winehouse have put Croydon on the map because of the success of the BRIT School. Even though they're not originally from Croydon, they've been nurtured here, which should make everyone proud – I certainly am.'

However, Amy was ready to make her first big splash.

Chapter Three

SIMON SAYS

By this stage, Amy was singing regularly with the National Youth Jazz Orchestra. While performing with the orchestra, she was spotted by some very well-connected people. One of the people they were associated with was a certain Simon Fuller.

Fuller has been described in many different ways, some of them hysterically complimentary, some of them wildly derogatory. Born on 17 May 1960, Fuller has become perhaps the most important figure in the entertainment business. He has also been named by *Time* magazine as one of the hundred most influential people in the world. 'My business is creating fame and celebrity, and I'm one of the best in the world. I know it to the finest detail.' Not half! He started off working at

Chrysalis, in publishing and then A&R. In the mid-1980s he discovered the artist Paul Hardcastle and branched out on his own at the age of just twenty-five. His first single with Hardcastle, '19', was a Number 1 hit and, off the back of the success, Fuller set up his own management company – calling it 19 Management.

Next, he discovered singer-songwriter Cathy Dennis and helped her to a string of worldwide smash hits during the 1990s. Then, he plucked Annie Lennox from her post-Eurythmics lull and relaunched her as a phenomenally successful solo artist. However, even these achievements were dwarfed by the success he had with the Spice Girls. He took over their management in 1996, and within months the band were a major success and their debut single, 'Wannabe', went to Number 1 in thirty-six countries. Next up, he launched S Club 7 who had eleven top-five singles in the UK. Ever with his eye on a dynasty, when the band split Fuller had a ready-made replacement – S Club Juniors.

Then came his move into television with *Pop Idol* and then *American Idol*. These shows smashed television viewing records and *American Idol* has gone on to become the most valuable TV format on the planet. Up to 74 million votes were cast during the *American Idol* final in 2007.

Fuller has also entered the sports world, guiding the careers of Steve McManaman and David Beckham. He owns the commercial rights to the name and images of Muhammad Ali and Elvis Presley's Graceland estate. Most recently, he has reunited with the Spice Girls to promote their reunion world tour. Worth £450 million, Fuller has been described as 'the man who wants to rule the world'. Well, if that's true then he's pretty close to realising his ambition.

For Amy's part, she was not a fan of Fuller's *Pop Idol* franchise. 'I never wanted any of this and that's the truth,' she says of her fame, adding, 'I would have been happy to sing in a covers band for the rest of my life. And I wouldn't have gone on one of those shows in a million billion years, because I think that musicality is not something other people should judge you on. Music's a thing you have with yourself. Even though the people who go on those shows are shit, it's really damaging to be *told* that you are.'

There are conflicting reports on how Amy came to Fuller's attention. One story has it that Sylvia Young arranged for two of his colleagues to come and watch her perform with the National Youth Jazz Orchestra; the other has it that James, who was already signed up to a subsidiary of 19 Management called Brilliant 19, put a word in for her with his managers.

Whatever the case, once at Brilliant 19, Amy was managed by Nick Godwin. A sharp music man, Godwin had been involved with the Spice Girls. He followed the tried-and-tested Brilliant 19 path of honing and nurturing talent. Amy had not long since stopped working as an entertainment journalist, writing for a music magazine and a fledgling showbiz news agency. Now, however, she was ready to step onto the other side of the showbiz divide.

Amy puts the link with 19 down to her friend Tyler James. 'I had one gig with the National Jazz Orchestra and my friend

Tyler, he was with his A&R guy Nicky [Shamansky], and Nicky said to him, "I heard this girl singing jazz on the radio," and Nicky said, "Well my friend Amy sings jazz and she's great." I think I must have been about sixteen. So I think Nicky was the one who convinced me to make a tape.'

As with the BRIT School, Amy is now keen to distance herself somewhat from the 19 Management experience. 'I met Simon Fuller, like, two times!' she once sighed when an interviewer asked her about her involvement with him. Indeed, she once also claimed that the extent of Fuller's involvement with her was that he happened to share a building with her management company Brilliant 19. In fact, Fuller funded that company. When asked what impression he made on her, she says haughtily, 'Businesspeople don't leave an impression with me. They go out of my head straightaway.'

When pressed on her time under Fuller's guidance, she says, 'It was never right. My manager on paper was not the person doing the day-to-day stuff. He was a lovely fellow but he didn't care about music. He was definitely one of those people who left their work in the office. I needed someone else. I needed someone who really cared.'

However, Fuller insists, 'Music is my first love. I have hundreds and hundreds of CDs! And I understand it. Music is a positive force.' Fuller was said to be horrified by Amy's increasingly bitchy remarks about other artists, including Madonna, of whom she said, 'She's an old lady. She should get a nice band, just stand in front of them and fucking sing.' Reportedly, he was unimpressed by her bitchy remarks about other pop stars, including his artist Rachel Stevens. A source said, 'Amy is under the wing of *Pop Idol*'s Simon Fuller and he is upset about her remarks on his stars.' Was she under pressure to sell a certain number of records? 'I don't think he cares if he gets a return on me. He's got *Pop Idol* and his empire. He's a smart man.' Amy has also been asked whether she was *really* uninterested in making money at this stage of her career. 'No. Well, I am. Everyone's interested in money. But if someone offered me three million pounds to make a Rachel Stevens cover record, I'd take it. Ha-ha! No.'

'When I was eighteen, I wasn't banging their door down. I didn't go out looking to be famous,' she says. 'I'm just a musician.' Her designated manager at 19 admitted at the time, 'She can be very frustrating. But I don't have an issue with her frankness,' he says. 'She's a real artist who's going to make records for years to come, someone passionate who speaks their mind and isn't interested in money.' In 2006, she and Fuller parted company and she took up Raye Cosbert as her new manager.

Before long, Amy had signed her first record deal with Universal/Island Records. Darcus Beese was the label's A&R man who signed her and he says his rivals were 'gutted' to miss out on Amy. Beese was of course jubilant and arranged to show off his new acquisition to the great and the good of his company. Amy played an acoustic set in the boardroom of Universal/Island. As she sat down in the posh leather seats, she nervously clipped her hair back, politely declining an offer of a glass of water. Then her nerves dispersed as she launched into a smooth, acoustic offering of 'There Is No Greater Love'.

At the end of the song, she received a rapturous round of applause from the music executives, who were delighted to have such a potentially profitable artist on their books. They could see the pound signs in front of their very eyes.

The artist known as John the White Rapper remembers meeting Amy around this time and being blown away by both her personality and voice. 'Once there, I didn't really say much to be honest, but Amy was singing and I remember being shocked – I'd never heard anybody sing so beautifully so close to me; all I could talk about when we walked home was getting her into the studio.' Their friendship was swiftly declared. 'After that we started to hang out. I was a bit of a nice guy, really. I'd go round and there'd be mess like you would not believe – piles of washing-up everywhere – and I hate mess so I used to wash up. I think that's what made her love me.'

Again, though, Amy wasn't seeing things quite the same way. Her father Mitch says that, to the laid-back Amy, signing up with Universal/Island was 'just her way of getting her music out'. Amy confirms this: 'I honestly never thought I would make any money from music – I figured I'd get a job in an office or as a waitress. I never had a great plan or promoted myself, but in a way I've been working for this for years.' She recalls her sense of puzzlement when it first all took off for her. 'He [Nicky Shamansky] said to me, "Do you want some studio time?" and I was so green around the gills I was just, like, "For what?" He said, "Well, if you write songs with your guitar and make a record, you'll get a record deal." I was like, "Really? What do you get out of it?" I guess I'm a very lucky girl.'

How typical of Amy – to think she was the lucky one in the equation. To the outsider, the lucky people in this equation were the record company who captured the talent of this extraordinary young woman. Lucky, too, were the listeners who would get to hear her wonderful songs. However, Amy has always put music ahead of not just fame but also ego. In any case, with her signature secured on the contract, the next step for her record label was to get her to put out a record. And what a wonderful yet controversial record it was to prove to be!

Chapter Four

TO BE FRANK

As Mitchell Winehouse drove his taxi around London in the autumn of 2003, he saw posters with his daughter's face on them. The posters were promoting her new album, *Frank*. Released on 23 October 2003, *Frank* is an album of relentless contradictions. Not only did its musical styles and lyrical themes often contrast with each other, so did much of the wider story of the album, which was spoken of more highly by many reviewers than it was by Amy herself.

It was produced mainly by the renowned hip-hop producer Salaam Remi, who was a fantastic man to have at the controls. Best known for his work with the American rapper Nas, Remi has produced such commercial tunes as Ini Kamoze's 'Here Comes the Hotstepper' and the Fugees's multi-platinum album *The Score*. He has also worked with Ms Dynamite, Toni Braxton and Lauryn Hill.

Hill's debut album has been cited by Amy as having had a huge influence on her as a youngster. She is also a huge fan of Nas, telling one interviewer, 'I am Nas's biggest fan. He's my favourite. I've been in the club when he's walked in and I've had a panic attack and had to walk out. It's like Michael Jackson, *Bad*-era hysteria.' For *Frank*, Remi was at the controls for the majority of the tunes and also played bass on some of the tracks.

Despite having such a star-studded CV, he does not have a huge celebrity presence of his own – quite deliberately. He explains, 'I didn't want to be seen as a public figure. An industry person, cool – most people in the industry over five or six years, I have crossed paths with them, because I have been around that long, so all the presidents and senior VPs I have crossed paths with them by now, but I am not really or want to be a public figure. I like to be known by industry peers and people I work with, but I like the fact that I can walk around.'

Nor does the broad range of genres he works in ever cause him any confusion as he moves from artist to artist. Indeed, he believes it enhances his work. 'I think the fact that I listen to and work on different types of music keeps me fresh whenever I get back to whatever it is,' he says. 'A lot of the times, I create based on the project and the artist. It's not like I'm just making it just for making it's sake; sometimes I do that, but I'll get into Amy Winehouse, and I won't be thinking about what I did for Shabba Ranks. It's different, but, say, on the Amy Source album, there's a cover of "Moody's Mood for Love", which is a jazz song by James Moody and King Pleasure, and we made that into a Reggae song. So [with] me having different influences, I can mix it. But I also keep them separate just by working around the artist's project at hand, whatever's needed.'

Expanding on his methodology, Remi said, 'I am concerned with songs that are going to stick and that takes a vehicle, great lyrics that are going to stick, that is when you're going to get a classic album overall. I really get in and work with people and work on a lot of music if I have my choice and, even if someone only wants to do one song, I'm, like, "Let's do four and you can pick the best one off it." '

One of the songwriters Amy had worked with on the album was Felix Howard. He told music critic Garry Mulholland that the beginning of their songwriting partnership was amusing. 'He told me that, the first time she turned up at his studio to write with him, she picked up her battered old acoustic guitar and started playing this song that just lasted for ever and ever and ever,' reveals Mulholland. 'Felix had to say, "Stop! Maybe you could sing "Sad-Eyed Lady of the Lowlands" [a hellishly indulgent Bob Dylan track] in five years' time when you have an audience!" He said she was just on her own planet. She'd no interest in what the market was looking for. Her instincts have to be reined in by the producers and songwriters she works with. She'd probably be writing fifteen- or twenty-minute-long folk odysseys with no chorus.'

Frank was recorded in Miami, where Remi has quite a setup. 'My main studio is in Miami in my home,' he says. 'Every room in my house has something musical. I have ridiculous amounts of equipment. I call my house Instrument Zoo.' Among the musicians to work with Amy on the album were guitarists Binky Griptite and Thomas Brenneck, drummers Troy Auxilly-Wilson and Homer Steinweiss, saxophonists Andy Mackintosh, Chris Davies, Jamie Talbot, Mike Smith and Neal Sugarman and pianist John Adams. Handclaps were provided by Vaughan Merrick, Mark Ronson and Victor Axelrod. The sound effects were generated by American producer, rapper and actor RZA. Aside from two cover versions, Amy co-wrote or, in the case of 'I Heard Love is Blind', wrote every track on the album.

So what did the album actually sound like? With its smoky, jazzy sound, opener 'Stronger Than Me' is a lament of the new man. Amy addresses a man who is seven years older than she is but refuses to play a masculine, leading role in a relationship. Instead, he wants to talk things through with her and put her in control. He wants her to meet his mother but she just wants to have sex with him and asks since when did that become a crime? As a result of all this, Amy has forgotten the joy that love can bring. She's tired of comforting him and wants him to comfort her. At one point, she even asks if he is gay. In the *Observer Music Monthly*, the excellent Garry Mulholland was outraged and delighted in equal measure. He wrote how 'liberal, reconstructed, ex-student males' had for so long been adored by the female singer-songwriter, 'and then this Jewish teenager from Camden comes along and tells us we're just a bunch of poofs.'

Mulholland identifies how, to Amy, a man 'showing his sensitive side is about as sexy as setting light to his farts'. However, he adores 'the subtle, soulful music and a voice so assured, joyful and deeply committed in its anger it's hard to believe it comes from one so young'. He concludes rousingly, that 'My worldview is threatened by it. Which means it is doing what pop ought to do – putting its head above the parapet: "This is what I really feel, so fuck you." ' Some wondered if Amy was homophobic, thanks to lines about a 'ladyboy' and her asking whether her lover is gay. Given her enthusiastic interviews with the gay press and appearances at gay venues, it seems unlikely. Moreover, her target with these lines is wimpy straight boys, rather than gay men. Also worth noting is that, when Kelly Osbourne once asked Amy if she considered herself a pin-up, Amy quipped, 'Only to gays.'

Talking of the song herself, Amy said, 'Some of the songs, like "Stronger Than Me" [which castigates an oversensitive paramour] were written at a time in my life when I was too [messed] up to do anything apart from write songs – when I felt I would have gone crazy and smashed my room up.' A fan, Jo-Ann Hodgson, wrote on a fan site:

> She stands out as having real songwriting talent and a strong soulful voice in a music scene being overtaken by impostors. This song takes the unusual angle of a woman asking her boyfriend to toughen up.

Amy says:,

> The gay thing was me just wanting some affection. It's not
> like I need to be the centre of attention all the time. But if
> my man comes round and turns on the TV, unless it's
> football I'm like, 'Are you even attracted to me?' They're
> very personal and very intense, in a way. But I think
> there's a lot of humour in there as well. I've always wanted
> to present a point with a twist. You know, like 'I'm really
> angry about this, you're a bastard and you can't even get a
> boner!' I just want to say things I would find funny if I
> heard them.

'You Sent Me Flying' is a beautiful piano ballad detailing a
rejection that sent Amy flying. Full of familiar Amy imagery
about stolen cigarettes, battered jeans and Beastie Boys T-
shirts, it blends the theme of heartbreak with a rousing
defiance. Towards the song's end, Amy explains that she isn't
actually as into the man as she might appear to be and the
music goes uptempo to reflect this comforting and defiant
reflection. She also comforts herself that he delivered the news
in a kind way and, well, at least he was attracted to her.

Tagged on the end of 'You Sent...' is 'Cherry', a short and fun
guitar song in which Amy talks about how her friend Cherry
understands her better than her man does. Cherry, though, is
her new guitar, whose every sound Amy loves. Perhaps, she
reflects, if her man were made of wood and strings then the
two could have as good a relationship as she enjoys with

Cherry. It's a fun, light-hearted song and picks up the mood of the album.

'Know You Now' is a light and easy tune set to jazzy guitar with background flute and bird song. Amy does some fantastic ad-libs towards the song's close and her vocal performance on this track is reminiscent of Mary J Blige.

Then comes another of the album's standout tracks 'Fuck Me Pumps'. Co-written with Salaam Remi and conceived by him, this is a simple but catchy tune and a strong live favourite. The lyric concerns the wannabe footballers' wives who are prevalent in much of twenty-first-century nightlife. At times Amy is scathing of them, saying they all look the same, and then mocks them for losing their charm as they approach thirty. She also identifies their hypocrisy in that they claim not to be chasing footballers but clearly are. However, as the song progresses, Amy has kinder words for them. Without such people, she declares, there would be no fun nightlife to be had. This is very much a twenty-first-century song, not just for the trend it identifies but also for its contemporary references to boob jobs and text messages. It's jazz for the *Heat* magazine generation. 'I have, like, pairs of them,' she said about her penchant for high heels. 'I'm a hypocrite in a way, because I'm poking fun in the song, but that's all I wear.'

When it was released as a single, the title was changed to the more radio-friendly 'F Me Pumps'. She says, 'Well, the single's actually "Fuck Me Pumps" with "Help Yourself" on the other side of it. In the video I mouth the words "Fuck me", but they took the audio out in the edit! The first time I saw it I was, like,

"Fuck! Where's my 'fuck'? I say 'fuck' there!" I'd love them to run it on *CD:UK* with the "fuck" in. But they won't.'

One line in the song uses the word 'sket' and Amy was once asked what this word means. 'A sket is like a dirty, pikey girl. Say you're with your little brother who's thirteen and you see a ratty little girl who you know. He'll go "I really like that girl," and you'll go "Please don't go anywhere near her, she's a right sket." She's a girl who's manky. Manky inside.'

'I Heard Love Is Blind' is two minutes and ten seconds of Amy soulfully pleading for forgiveness for cheating on her man. Set to a simple tune of acoustic guitar and flute, the song's lyric details a moment of infidelity Amy committed when left alone by her man. However, she pleads, she wasn't really cheating on her man because she was thinking of him when she came and the man she slept with looked like her boyfriend in any case. Surely he wouldn't want her to be lonely – and she didn't let the man hold her hand. 'I believe in casual sex,' Amy said while discussing this song. 'I know it's sad that I think cheating on people is fine. But I think it's like smoking a spliff. Oops, I've gobbed on meself!'

'There Is No Greater Love' is a cover of an Isham Jones number and joins 'Moody's Mood for Love' as a great nod to the artists who have influenced and thrilled Amy. However, the classic sound of both tunes is contrasted sharply by the next song on the album – 'In My Bed'. With a trip-hop beat and contemporary production, this song is also far longer than many of the others on the album. She is seen singing this song acoustically on the documentary included on the DVD *I Told*

You I Was Trouble. At five minutes and seventeen seconds, it far outlasts the likes of 'I Heard...' (two minutes and ten seconds) and 'Know You Now' (three minutes and three seconds).

The song amounts to an ultimatum from Amy to her boyfriend. She wants him to separate sex from emotion but fears he is unable to do this. She feels their relationship has gone stale and there is nothing new for her to learn. She has to look away when they make love because everything is so familiar and to her that's not a good thing. She concludes that, unless he agrees to see and approach things her way, then her way will be a different way – away from him. She also memorably points out that she holds his hand only to, ahem, help him get the angle right.

'Take the Box' details the drama of a break-up. A mournful jazz song, it was chosen as a single and charted highest of all the album's singles. During the song she hands back the presents her man gave her, including a Frank Sinatra album and a Moschino bra. As the break-up becomes more traumatic, even the neighbours get dragged into the drama. Such public laundry washing would become true in the future for Amy, of course. She concludes that someone who up until this day was beautiful has turned ugly in her eyes because of something awful he has said. This was selected as a stand-out track by many reviewers, including that of the *Guardian*.

With an infectious funky guitar riff and hip-hop percussion, 'October Song' features a surprisingly mature vocal performance, even by Amy's widely admired standards. Managing to produce an upbeat jazz track out of the death of her pet canary, Amy shows a heartbreakingly sweet side to her character here. She consoles herself that her pet Ava has flown to paradise.

A dark, soulful wah-wah guitar line dominates 'What Is It About Men?'. Amy mourns that she has at times chosen the wrong man in her life. She feels she does this as naturally as she sings. She says her destructive side is growing and asks herself repeatedly: what is it about men? This track has been described by the *Observer* as 'a sneery examination of said subject which is quite obviously about her dad and his romantic entanglements'. As for Amy, she confirmed the links with her dad. 'It's me trying to work out my dad's problems with sticking with one woman, trying to make sense of why he did certain things. I completely understand it now. People like to have sex with people. I don't begrudge my dad just because he has a penis. What's the point?'

For his part, Mitchell is philosophical about Amy's wanton laundering of dirty linen. 'I think it's only the first part that's specifically about me,' he says. 'The rest of it is more generally about what rats men are. But the song's given me pause for thought, because the divorce obviously coloured her view of men.'

'Help Yourself' can best be seen as a sister track to 'Stronger Than Me'. Again, Amy is berating her man for not being strong enough. She is tired of carrying him and having to hold his head above water for him. She cannot help him unless he is equally willing to help himself. Although her lover is twenty-five years old, she sees him more as a sixteen-year-old. His degree in philosophy doesn't impress her one bit because where you are now is far more important than where you have been. Again, Amy is fair and stresses that she has walked in her lover's shoes and so understands his dilemma. All the same, she's had enough of the situation as it stands.

And so the album concludes with 'Amy, Amy, Amy', thirteen minutes and fourteen seconds of Cuban-flavoured, swinging ode to the joys of her man and the frustrations of how his sex appeal distracts her from her songwriting craft. An announcer thanks everyone for coming and says he hopes we enjoyed it. We did.

Clocking in at just twelve seconds short of an hour's listening, *Frank* certainly lived up to its title. From her asking her lover if he's gay in the opening track to her open admissions of sexual urging in the final track, it is sharp and to the point. It is also, as Amy revealed while promoting the album, largely based on the experiences she had with one lover. 'He's a very proud man and I know he won't go and buy the album,' she said. 'We were together when I'd written some stuff, but I don't think he's listened to some of the less flattering songs I wrote later on. He did say to me, "How would you feel if I did this to you?" But I was, like, "What? Someone you once loved has written a really nice album about you." Then he said, "Amy, you called me gay!" So I told him, "I didn't say you were gay, I just put the question out there. Are you?" He's just being a baby because someone wrote an album about him. His mates are all probably really jealous.'

Already, therefore, Amy was setting out her stall as an artist who was willing to be open and honest in both her lyrics and in interviews. In an age when pop acts are often trained in how to be evasive and squeaky clean in their image, Amy's frankness was a breath of fresh air.

However, some wondered, would potential lovers feel quite so enamoured by her openness? 'Yeah, I'm an open book,' she agreed. 'Some men do think I'm a psycho bunny-boiler. But I think that's funny. If you're nice to me I'll never write anything bad about you. There's no point in saying anything but the truth. Because, at the end of the day, I don't have to answer to you, or my ex, or... I shouldn't say God... or a man in a suit from the record company. I have to answer to myself.'

So we return to the contradictions that dominate the album. At one point she castigates a lover for being unfaithful but elsewhere she also criticises him for being *too* faithful. She complains about finding it hard to find a man but then also mourns that she so often picks the *wrong* man. Nor is it just the words that are at odds with each other. The music is wonderfully old-fashioned and yet the cultural references – text messages, Beastie Boys T-shirts – are firmly rooted in the twenty-first century. 'It's different. A break from the same old shit,' she says of her own music. 'It's important to be a great singer. [But] it's important for me to stand out and be different and do something different and say something different.'

Perhaps the most intriguing aspect of *Frank* is the fact that Amy has as good as disowned it. Her official website had the following to say about the album: '*Frank* was her grand and suitably blunt-speaking break-up record, and it won her a battalion of fans around the world, marking her out as one of the most distinct new voices in pop; confessional, elemental and with that rarest of combinations: humour and soul.'

So far, so complimentary. However, as soon as she was unleashed in front of journalists, Amy said she was 'only 80 per cent' behind the album. 'I can't even listen to *Frank* any more – in fact, I've never been able to,' she confessed to a shocked interviewer. 'I like playing the tracks live because that's different, but listening to them is another story.

'Some things on this album make me go to a little place that's fucking bitter. I've not seen anyone from the record company since the album came out. And I know why. They're scared of me and they know I have no respect for them whatsoever.'

It was the way that the album positioned her in a place she didn't want to be that helped inform her distaste of it. For a start, it saw her bracketed by Katie Melua and Jamie Cullum. 'People put us together because we have come out at the same time, but we're nothing alike,' she says. 'I feel bad for Jamie, being lumped in with me and her. I'm a songwriter and she has her songs written for her. He must feel frustrated. *She* must think it's her fucking lucky day. If anyone stands out straight from us, it would be her,' she continues of Katie Melua, because she doesn't write her own songs. 'It's not like she's singing old songs like Jamie, she's singing shit new songs that her manager writes for her.'

Amazingly, she claims that not only does she not listen to

Frank, but, 'I've never heard the album from start to finish. I don't have it in my house. The marketing was fucked, the promotion was terrible. Everything was a shambles. It's frustrating, because you work with so many idiots – but they're nice idiots. So you can't be, like, "You're an idiot." They know that they're idiots.' So disillusioned was she that she wasn't to write another song for eighteen months.

So, not the most enthusiastic words about the album from Amy herself. However, the response from the critics was far, far more complimentary. The BBC website said that the album was 'Lyrically fresh and uncompromising'. It added, 'This is Amy's first release and augurs well for her future. If this is what the young lady is capable of at such an early stage it must be pretty certain that this will be the first in a long line of well crafted, funky & feisty releases.' In the *Guardian*, Beccy Lindon wrote, 'Sitting somewhere between Nina Simone and Erykah Badu, Winehouse's sound is at once innocent and sleazy... It's hard not to hear the honesty and soul that resonates throughout this album.'

In *The Times*, Paul Connolly concluded that,

Her *Frank* could not be more aptly titled, with its dissection of romantic farragos, sexual betrayal and jealousy, peppered with caustic put-downs and killer one-liners. 'F*** Me Pumps', a withering attack on women of a certain age who hit the town in search of a rich husband but end up with a string of one-night stands, is beyond acerbic. Its cutting lyrics – 'Like the news, every day you get pressed' – are only marginally softened by a skinny tune that vaguely resembles 'Winter Wonderland'.

The *Evening Standard* profiled Amy to tie in with the release and said,

> That debut album, *Frank* (as in both her hero, Sinatra, and her disarming manner), is a remarkably assured cornucopia – part jazz, part hip-hop, but reminiscent of Norah Jones, Dinah Washington and, mostly, American soul diva Erykah Badu. It's accessible enough for Radio 2 to feature heavily; commercial enough for her to be signed by an offshoot of super-manager Simon Fuller's operation and sufficiently cutting-edge to have been granted nods of approval from magazines such as *Straight No Chaser* and *Blues Soul*.

The hip magazine *Dazed And Confused* said it was one of 'the most impressive British debuts in years'; *MOJO* gave it four out of five and described it as a 'stunning debut'. Elsewhere it was described as Nelly Furtardo meeting Billie Holiday.

The feminist writer Holly Combe says of the album's artwork,

> The image is of someone who likes all the apparent fripperies of Being-a-Girl but who knows how to keep up with The Lads too. In other words, we're talking about the perfectly balanced image. Just like the much sought after

'mostly B's' archetype in those quizzes in *Cosmo* and *Just Seventeen*. Nice one Amy!

The *Leicester Mercury* was less approving, saying, 'In fact it's intense, maybe a little too much so. Although this is the album that may make her name, it's not the one to carve it into the Hall of Fame. But time and a blossoming vocal talent are on her side.' It seems that other local press in the Midlands was not enthusiastic, either. The *Birmingham Evening Mail* said, 'Her Macy Gray-style voice is an acquired taste, however.' The Metacritic website – which collates all reviews of albums and gives them an 'overall rating' – gave *Frank* 84/100.

The album entered the UK charts at Number 60 but had climbed to its peak position of Number 13 by January 2004. It was to re-enter the charts when Amy's profile was raised by the release of her following album, *Back to Black*. It made Number 28 in the Irish charts. As good as disowned by Amy and a slow-burner initially in the charts due to a lack of radio play, *Frank* nonetheless remains a classic album and one that swept Amy to the attention of the music industry.

It also earned Amy her first serious nomination for an award. The Mercury Prize is an annual music prize awarded for the best album from the United Kingdom or Republic of Ireland, established as an alternative to the industry-dominated BRIT Awards. The nominees are chosen by a selected panel of executives in the music industry in the UK and the Republic of Ireland. The Mercury Prize also has a reputation for being awarded to outside chances rather than the favourites. 'The point of the Mercury is not simply to elect a winner: the point of the Mercury is to give publicity to and celebrate all sorts of music,' says Simon Frith, chairman of the judging panel. Previous winners included Ms Dynamite, M People and Talvin Singh. Frith added that the panel have never got the choice wrong.

The other nominees for the 2004 prize were Basement Jaxx (*Kish Kash*), Belle & Sebastian (*Dear Catastrophe Waitress*), Franz Ferdinand (*Franz Ferdinand*), Jamelia (*Thank You*), Keane (*Hopes and Fears*), Snow Patrol (*Final Straw*), Joss Stone (*The Soul Sessions*), the Streets (*A Grand Don't Come for Free*), Ty (*Upwards*), Robert Wyatt (*Cuckooland*), and the Zutons (*Who Killed... The Zutons?*).

At the ceremony on 8 September 2004, the award went to Scottish indie rockers Franz Ferdinand. 'This is coming in a year when we're surrounded by such fantastic bands,' said the band's charming lead singer Alex Kapranos. 'Everyone else deserves it more than we do. They reflect a trend in the UK at the moment for fantastic music so we're living in pretty good times at the moment.' Bless him! Amy may not have won but she did perform at the ceremony and she'd be back before long. Indeed, little could she have known then quite how many awards she would go on to be nominated for, or how many of them she would win.

Also in 2004, Amy was nominated for two BRIT awards. The categories she was shortlisted in were British Female Solo Artist and British Urban Act. The ceremony was at Earls Court and hosted by Cat Deeley, who appeared wearing a top hat and straddling a huge champagne bottle, declaring, 'Booze is back! Rock and roll is back!' Amy would have approved. The evening was dominated by the glam rockers the Darkness, who won three awards. Busted and Justin Timberlake were double winners, and Beyoncé Knowles took the award for Best International Female. Laughter erupted across the arena when DJ Chris Moyles said, 'I'm sitting backstage – it's rubbish. I've got to look at Dr Fox's fat face all night. No food, no booze, no birds – it's rubbish.'

On the night Amy won neither award with the British Female Solo Artist gong going to Dido. Accepting her award via a video message, she said she was 'pretty surprised' to have won. 'I know it's voted for by the public, I'm so grateful.' Meanwhile the British Urban act award was handed to Lemar, who had come to prominence from the BBC's *Fame Academy* programme.

By this time, Amy had performed her first major headline show in London. Billed as 'an attractive oasis on Shepherd's Bush's busy Uxbridge Road', Bush Hall is one of the capital's most charismatic venues. At the start of the twentieth century, it hosted ballroom dancing, swing orchestras and Irish music jigs. Then, during World War Two, it became a soup kitchen for hungry locals, before becoming a bingo hall and then an amusement arcade in the postwar years. During the 1990s it became a snooker hall, which was visited by famous people, including Hugh Grant and Stephen Fry. At the start of the twenty-first century it was renovated and has since hosted concerts for a host of acts, including REM, Boy

George – his first concert for over a decade – Scissor Sisters, Lily Allen and Sugababes.

The venue has a capacity of 350 and much of that was, on the evening, made up of curious music industry folk and friends of Amy. With space at such a premium on and off the stage, Amy had to fight for performing room with her band, particularly the brass section. She opened with 'Best Friends' and soon had the audience enchanted as she proceeded to 'You Sent Me Flying' and 'Know You Now'. 'I'm really snotty tonight,' said Amy at one point, wearing a black strapped top and leopard-print leggings.

Caroline Sullivan wrote in her review for the *Guardian*: 'Most impressive when it was just her and a guitarist, as on "(There is) No Greater Love", Winehouse is the very definition of "potential"... long may her angst unfurl.'

Writing in *The Times*, Lisa Verrico agreed with Sullivan that Amy was at her best without the brass section, saying she was 'simply compelling' when accompanied by just her guitarist. She also echoed Sullivan's praise of her performance of 'There Is...', writing of 'gasps from the audience' during the song. As Amy turned to 'Stronger Than Me', the audience was full of moving hips and wide smiles. It had been a successful night, with even Amy's between-song chatter raising some chuckles in the assembled throng. A successful evening, then: Amy impressed reviewers, music industry figures and her fans. Not bad for a night's work.

A concert at Northumbria University followed. *Newcastle Evening Chronicle* reviewer Claire Dupree wrote,

The first thing that strikes you about Amy is how can such a powerful voice come from someone so tiny? Her voice belies her age and her husky North London accent is transformed into a sultry jazzy drawl. The music has an almost big band feel at times and encompasses an excellent brass section. A particular favourite, 'You Sent Me Flying', reduced a previously noisy crowd to silence with emotive lyrics about unrequited love. [The lyrics,] which sent shivers down my spine, gave me goosebumps and sent the crowd into frenzied applause.

Not that all reviews were favourable at this point. For instance, Fiona Shepherd, writing in the *Scotsman* about Amy's performance at the Cottier Theatre in Glasgow, tore strips off her performance in general and vocal accomplishments in particular. She said Amy's style,

was tedious after five minutes, let alone an hour and five minutes, and her rich, mature tone was poorly served by her favoured vocal style. Winehouse oversang mercilessly like just another competent *Pop Idol* wannabe, mistaking vocal acrobatics for sophisticated soulful interpretation. By the time she had finished mangling each track, any melody which might have asserted itself was totally exterminated.

She soon was to perform in Dublin, where the *Irish Times* reviewer wrote,

There is still less doe-eyed sentimentality, or disingenuous coyness, in Winehouse's music, a sassy mix of purring jazz and growling hip-hop to match her earthy, booty-shaking sexuality. We are a little taken aback, nonetheless, to find the recent Ivor Novello Award winner on stage this muggy evening, tugging at her neckline and blowing down her dress. Picking up where the venue's air-conditioning falls short, it's typical Winehouse: balancing moments of cool relief with music that's resolutely hot 'n' bothered.

A more eccentric write-up surfaced in *Newsquest*, following her show at the Liverpool Academy. Ian Kelly wrote,

She is an amazingly charismatic live performer and, despite looking like the lovechild of Penelope Cruz and Ruud van Nistelrooy, she is also very sexy. And this girl really knows how to carry a tune. This was a note-perfect display of her unquestionable vocal talents which was absolutely stunning.

Amy's performance at the 2004 T in the Park festival was not quite so well written up. The *Daily Star*'s Joe Mott wrote, 'Her mesmerising vocals are spoiled by a crowd that thinks it's in the theatre and chats throughout.'

She also turned out at Warwick University, University of Northumbria, the Brecon Annual Jazz Festival, the Harrogate International Jazz Festival, Ross-on-Wye International Festival and the Montreal International Jazz Festival. Jordan Zivitz wrote in the *Montreal Gazette*, 'Winehouse left her hip-hop beats at home, singing with a trio that left her barbed lyrics and modern-day Billie Holiday vocals plenty of room to move.'

After watching her a second time, Zivitz added,

> We did, however, get a powerhouse voice that more than lived up to Winehouse's promise on the album, and a coolly measured stage presence that made her spiky lyrics seem all the more dangerous. The revised instrumentation gave the material a more traditionally jazzy feel than on the hip-hop-inflected *Frank* CD – more deep indigo than flaming red. Whatever the colour, Winehouse is going places. Among those places, no doubt, is a larger venue than Club Soda next time.

Within days of performing at Montreal, Amy turned out at Cannizaro Park at Merton and in London's Old Street, where she had trouble remembering the lyrics. 'She actually said, "I have to try and remember this shit now," ' says one audience member. 'That's not exactly a very good plug for her new material.' She also put in an appearance at Pizza Express Jazz Club in 2004. The *Guardian* review gave a drenchingly positive write-up:

> Amy Winehouse joined for the second half, mixing singles from her album *Frank* with jazz standards including 'Caravan' and 'What a Difference a Day Makes'. Her timing and inflection come from hip-hop, contemporary soul and R&B rather than jazz – but an improviser's

instincts often made her swim spectacularly upstream against the undercurrents.

However, it was the *Daily Telegraph*'s report that best captured the drama of the evening. Neil McCormick wrote,

> Freed from having to concentrate on her own guitar-playing, she really shone as a vocalist, while the trio jazzed up her songs (and a sprinkling of classic covers) with genuine brio. Highlight of the evening, however, was when Winehouse's oft-mentioned dad, singing taxi-driver Mitchell Winehouse, took over for a smooth rendition of a Frank Sinatra song. Confidently demonstrating the genetic root of Amy's talent, Mitch seemed unimpressed by some of the trio's experimental trimmings. With all the casual menace of an *EastEnders* villain, he paused his performance to inquire of the fresh faced piano player: 'Was that the bridge, or are you just doodling about as usual?'

That told him!

Later on while recalling the night, McCormick wrote, 'I watched her perform in a Pizza Express with her father Mitch, a Sinatra-singing taxi driver, and met a loving family clearly proud of Winehouse's success.' Amy was winning a huge reputation as a live act at this point in her career. The *Daily Mirror* previewed a concert of hers thus:

> She has an incredible voice, a great talent and a real knack

for putting her foot in it. But frank comments about fellow performers aside, it is in the live arena that Amy has to be savoured. Madonna may, or may not, mime, but Amy has a voice of such intensity as to make Madge look like a karaoke singer.

Reviewing a concert of hers at the UEA Norwich, John Street wrote in *The Times*,

> To begin with, her voice seems almost to take her over, like a headstrong dog dragging its owner across muddy fields and flooded ditches. As the show proceeds, these vocal mannerisms tend to become repetitive, as if trapped in a single emotional and musical register. Her voice is at its best on the more tightly arranged songs, where the attention is on the detail: 'Stronger Than Me', 'What is it About Men?', or 'Help Yourself'. The swoops and dives, the half-checked angry bark, populate these numbers with a twisting trail of sensations.

Amy has always said that performing live is what it is 'all about' to her. 'I love being on tour, but I wish I could work off the crowd better; be more of a showman,' she says. 'For me, it's all about the songs, and I'm so busy concentrating on that, I'm not paying as much attention to the audience.'

Meanwhile, her growing reputation domestically was being echoed around the world. A Singapore newspaper wrote of Amy,

Sporting thick black eyeliner and singing songs like 'F***
Me Pumps', this London native is surely the genre's bad
girl. Although she sings in typical jazz-blues fashion, the
beats reflect mainstream hip-hop and R&B more than
scat or even soul.

However, it was at home that Amy's star was shining
brightest. Around this time, the *Observer Music Monthly*
dispatched a journalist to pen the first major feature on Amy.
Respected music critic Garry Mulholland landed the gig and
had several interview sessions with Amy for the feature.
During an interview with the author, he recalled the
experience fondly. 'She's a dream interviewee,' he says,
smiling. 'Firstly, because she's an unstoppable quote machine.
Secondly because she's a really lovely girl who is easy to get
along with, very warm. I was going through an incredibly
difficult period in my personal life at the time. When I turned
up to meet Amy I was not in the world's greatest place so I was
quite nervous. I thought, "If she's difficult in any way, I'm
going to find this quite hard."

'She was hugely revealing, incredibly honest, fantastic
company. She made what could have been a very difficult
situation into a very easy one. I was just very grateful to her for
that. We sat down in this restaurant in Camden Town and
proceeded to get incredibly drunk on sangria. Despite her
reputation, I was definitely outdrinking her two to one.'

A journalist who interviewed Amy in Canada remembers a
similar atmosphere. When Amy attempted to stretch out

across the seating in the restaurant, a waiter expressed his distaste, prompting Amy to moan loudly, 'You ever just want to go to McDonald's?'

She was once also rather frank to a journalist during an interview, often and ostentatiously yawning from the offset. 'Sorry, but it doesn't come naturally, talking about myself,' she said, following another yawn. 'I don't see what's important about it. No offence to you, but I could be at my nan's house right now. Or I could be waiting at home for the plumber to come and fix the washing machine.'

Even a telephone interviewer was not spared a moment of Amy drama. 'Sorry, I've just been having a wee,' said the then brazen twenty-year-old. Yes, Amy Winehouse was on the loo. 'I'm sorry. I do it all the time. Whenever I go to the toilet I take the phone with me.'

Then she asked her telephone interrogator, 'Have you had sex to my album? Do you know anyone who has? I'd love to know who has,' she said. 'That's the test of a wicked album. Ask all your friends if they've ever had sex to my album. That would be cool. It would mean people can totally be themselves with my music.'

Garry Mulholland expands on this theme. 'She came over to me as completely gauche, someone who just didn't care,' he says. 'She will say exactly what's on her mind. If it offends you or someone else, tough. At one point she was being so revealing about this guy she'd been out with, who was the subject of the songs on the first album. She started to say his name and talk about him in a lot of detail. I actually stopped the interview and said, "You know what? I really think you should stop because I could print his name and all these details. You'd really regret it, so I'm actually suggesting you stop."

'So I actually had to rein her in, whereas it's normally the other way round. With Amy I had to stop her because it didn't seem fair to this guy. She's similar to Pete Doherty: she doesn't have a self-censoring button. If I'd asked her the exact length and dimensions of her ex-boyfriend's penis, she would have told me. It was extraordinary.'

Mulholland has interviewed an entire galaxy of musical stars during his career, so where does Amy fit in to his experiences? 'She was the most honest interviewee I've ever sat down with,' he says, 'and it didn't seem to be contrived shock tactics. She wasn't bitchy, it was just as if she was sitting talking to her best friend about sex.'

He insists that her honesty and openness is on a different level from that displayed by certain other artists, such as Robbie Williams. 'Robbie always comes across as someone who's constantly begging the public for sympathy. There's no self-pity in Amy's revelations. Her take on it is, "This happened and that happened and now I get to write great songs about it." When she's talking about things like sex, there's that "London girl" thing: a girl who can't resist blabbing about sex to everyone. But there's a tomboy element to it: she neither solicits your sympathy nor flirts with you. She never plays an "I'm a girl" game. She's bullish, forthright and assertive.'

Although back in 2004, Amy was far from the celebrity she

is today, Mulholland recalls that she already had that elusive quality: the X factor. 'She got up and went to the loo, it was a Jessica Rabbit moment,' he says. 'Literally everyone in this restaurant just turned round and watched her wriggle along this restaurant. It was more than sex: it was charisma. People didn't know who she was, so it wasn't to do with fame. It was pure lust and fascination.'

Charisma she had plenty of, and she had just as much eccentricity, says Mulholland. 'When we did the second interview, she turned up with these pink ballet shoes on. She looked like she'd stolen them off a tramp on the street. They were so worn down, they didn't even have toes on them any more. Once more, I thought, "This person is really on her own planet." She's a genuine eccentric, it's not contrived "I'm wild and crazy". Even if she hadn't got a record deal she would still be this insane girl who completely marches to the beat of her own drum. She was a sweetheart, even though she was quite obviously nuts.'

Even given her relative lack of fame at the time, Mulholland still found her to be enormously trusting. 'When I met her for the first interview, it was after a concert,' he recalls. 'We got in the cab and she said, "Actually, I've really got to take the guitar and the amp back home. Would you mind coming round to mine?" So we went back to her flat, in Camden Town, and it was just really sweet. I realised I was climbing the stairs to Amy Winehouse's home, carrying her guitar and amp. Her flat was perfectly nice, if a bit of a mess, as you might expect. How many other pop stars would invite a journalist to their home? It was just a very sweet gesture.'

In an interview with the author, respected author and cultural commentator Mark Simpson also contrasted Amy with Robbie Williams. 'She's the man that Robbie Williams dreams of being,' he said. 'Her tattoos are much better than his, and so is her wig. She'd wipe the floor with him in a pub fight. She wrote a song about not going to rehab – all his songs are about going to rehab. With his mum. It goes without saying that the voice is also much better. Even if Williams's voice actually got around to breaking, it wouldn't come close.'

Chris Cooke paints a similar portrait of the 'interviewing Amy' experience to the one Mulholland outlined: 'Was she a bit erratic during my interview? Well, yes, a bit – side conversations with her boyfriend and an assistant being sent out with dinner requirements did make the whole thing slightly hard to follow. But, at the same time, I would have been disappointed had it turned out any other way, because that's why we love Amy. And, while the slight yet harmless chaos made me sound like the dullest person on Earth when I tried to pull the conversation back on topic or sought a clarification or two, in amongst it all I think I managed to get the insight I wanted on the brilliant album that is *Back to Black*.'

She has also once fallen asleep during an interview with the hip US magazine *Blender*. When asked if she did drugs she told the interviewer Jody Rosen, 'I don't have the time.' Asked whether she was an alcoholic or not she said, 'I don't know. I'm a really big drinker. I used to be there before the pub opened, banging on the door.' She then began falling asleep, then saying,

'Oh, God! What is wrong with me? There's something wrong with me. I'm just really drowsy at the moment. I'm so sorry.'

Her interviewer said,

> Amy has never exactly been a picture of health, but tonight she looks especially worse for wear – hunched, heavy-lidded and just frail... Now her words are slurred, her eyelids drooping. Her head wobbles into a nod. She falls asleep for a second, wakes up with a start, mutters and drops off again. The smouldering cigarette in her left hand falls to the floor.

Another journalist, Aidan Smith, of *Scotland on Sunday*, expanded in his feature on Amy the 'bit of a mess' Mulholland hinted at in Amy's household. 'The fence is broken, a Yellow Pages rots by the gate, and empty cans of Stella litter the garden,' he wrote, and continued:

> Wading through the jumble of shoes in the hall, I reach the living-room. It looks like a crime scene, with mess everywhere: CDs and videos... discarded clothes – pants! – and half-drunk cups of coffee... a pair of giant comedy sunglasses and a cushion embroidered with a crude likeness of Patrick Swayze. I ignore the football in the corner; only a woman could live here.

Amy confirms the widespread tomboy perception of her when she says, 'I'm not really a girl. I'm not even a boy's girl.

I'm a man's man – and that doesn't mean I'm a big dyke. Men are far more straightforward. They don't dwell on things and play psychological games. I'm not saying all women are like that, or that some men don't play those games, but on the whole, men are more easygoing and don't piss time up the wall. Life's short. Anything could happen, and it usually does, so there's no point in sitting around thinking about all the ifs, ands and buts.'

Having come so close twice to winning a major award so early in her career, Amy hit the jackpot later in the year with arguably the most prestigious of musical honours. The Ivor Novello Awards were first given in 1955. Named after Ivor Novello, a Welsh composer, singer and actor who became one of the most popular British entertainers of the early twentieth century, the awards are now given by the British Academy of Composers and Songwriters. The Academy, formed in 1999, represents the interests of UK music writers across all genres. The Award itself is a solid bronze sculpture of Euterpe, the Greek muse of music. Former winners of this prestigious prize include Iron Maiden, the Darkness, the Feeling, Madonna, Freddie Mercury, Brian May, Richard Thompson, David Bowie, Ray Davies, Kate Bush, Eric Clapton, John Lennon, Annie Lennox, Phil Pickett, Paul McCartney, Madness, Duran Duran, George Michael, Pet Shop Boys, Dave Stewart, Sting, Robbie Williams and Gary Barlow.

She was delighted to be nominated for an Ivor Novello, far more than she was to be nominated Best Female at the BRITs. 'The Ivor Novellos are a songwriter's award and that's what I am,' she says. 'I'm not trying to be best female, I'm just trying to write songs.' However, in the wake of *Frank*'s success and Amy's disagreements with many aspects of the album and its promotion, she found writing songs more difficult than ever.

'I had writer's block for so long,' she says looking back. 'And, as a writer, your self-worth is literally based on the last thing you wrote... I used to think, "What happened to me?" At one point it had been two years since the last record and [the record company] actually said to me, "Do you even want to make another record?" I was, like, "I swear it's coming." I said to them, "Once I start writing I will write and write and write. But I just have to start it."

'I take out my anger and frustration by writing songs and that's really where *Frank* came from. And now I'm having a great time – everything is going really well with the record. I'm doing a lot of gigs and singing is the thing I love doing most. I'll have to start writing for a new album at some point, so I think I'm going to have to take time off and live a normal life so that things can happen to me again that aren't all good. Otherwise, I'll have nothing to write about on the next album.'

As we shall see, Amy's hope that normal things 'that aren't all good' would happen to her came true – but surely in a bigger way than she could ever have expected.

Chapter Five

BACK ON TRACK

When she returned to the public eye with her new album, Amy's hairstyle had moved towards the beehive style she is now synonymous with. From Holly Golightly in *Breakfast at Tiffany's*, to Bet Lynch in *Coronation Street*, to Marge in *The Simpsons*, to Patsy from *Absolutely Fabulous* through to most of the women in the cartoon *The Far Side*, the beehive hairstyle is a popular one. It originated in the 1950s when Margaret Vinci Heldt, a hairdresser from Elmhurst, Illinois, was asked to create a new style. 'It's kind of nice to know maybe in my own way I was able to give something to my profession that became a classic,' she said. 'It still has a touch of glamour, doesn't it?

'It was sort of the peak of hairdressing,' said Heldt.

'Everybody wanted the beehive, even women with real, real short hair. They looked more like anthills than a beehive then they got bigger and bigger and became hornets nests.'

'It really was the last great hairdo we've seen in thirty years,' adds Jackie Summers of *Modern Salon* magazine.

Meanwhile, UK *Vogue*'s fashion features writer Sarah Harris says, 'It is about fashion, owning a style, individuality and confidence, as well as success and talent. Not just with clothes but beauty, too. Amy Winehouse's hair has become as much a signature as her clothes.' Not just her signature, but an enduring mystery, too. 'Amy won't even tell her stylist, who also happens to be her best friend, what she does to get her hair like that,' says a friend. Amy's obsessed with her hair and only does it herself – it's been a huge secret.

Celebrity hairdresser Alex Foden, who designs and makes Amy's £150 hairpieces, cracks some of the mystery: 'Amy originally created the look herself but on a much smaller scale. But since I started working with her the beehive has simply got bigger and bigger – the bigger the better. Although she backcombed her own hair in the beginning, now we use furballs made from part synthetic, part real hair. These are stuffed inside hairnets and Amy's own hair is placed over the top of them and held in place with hairpins.

'It takes about forty minutes to fit a new hairpiece but only about five minutes to pin it up every morning once it's been made. The beehive is particularly big in the capital but is taking off everywhere as Amy becomes more popular. She is getting through one hairpiece a week at the moment so they are fairly high-maintenance, but as long as you do not sleep in one or go to the gym wearing one they can last a lot longer. As well as being very versatile, a taller, thinner beehive can alter the appearance of a person's natural body shape, adding height and making the face and body look leaner.'

It has very much caught on, too. 'Amy Winehouse has a lot to answer for!' laughs Lorraine Ellis, manager at the Hair Spa in Thornton Hall Hotel in Thornton Hough. 'But big hair is a really key trend this season and that means everything from the beehive look with a high crown, like Amy's, to a 1980s wavy style that Coleen's [McLoughlin, Wayne Rooney's fiancée] been seen with of late. That's a great look because you can wear it in the day and keep it quite soft using heated rollers, and then use Velcro rollers and tongs to glam it up a bit for night.'

The period between *Frank* and *Back to Black* is shrouded in mystery. Amy says, 'I started drinking and I fell in love.'

And she wrote a great album.

Back to Black has a dark name and a dark background. 'I was very hurt by something but I managed to make something good out of a bad situation,' says Amy. 'I think when I wrote *Back to Black* I was left in a situation where I wasn't working, and when I split up with this fellow I didn't have anything to go back to. I guess when you pick up the pieces from a relationship you go back to what you know and try to throw yourself into something. And I had nothing – I wasn't working. So I was just playing pool every day, getting drunk.'

While playing pool, Amy was filling the jukebox of her local pub with coins and the music she heard inspired her to write new songs. Shirley Bassey and the Angels were among the acts she was listening to but, as ever, the Shangri-Las were an inspiration. 'I know there are people in the world who have worse problems than falling in love and having it blow up in your face,' she said of the problems she was encountering with her boyfriend Blake at this time. 'But I didn't want to just wake up drinking, and crying, and listening to the Shangri-Las, and go to sleep, and wake up drinking, and listening to the Shangri-Las. So I turned it into songs, and that's how I got through it.

'I think all the stuff I was listening to, like a lot of doo-wop, a lot of sixties soul, Motown, girl groups, I tend to be influenced by whatever I'm listening to, so I think, I guess it's all stuff from the jukebox from when I used to go and play pool in the pub. It's jukebox music.'

It was here that Amy developed her own cocktail. She calls it the Rickstasy, and the drink consists of three parts vodka, one part Southern Comfort, one part banana liqueur, and one part Bailey's. 'By the time you've had two of them you're like, "Don't even try and go anywhere. Sit down and stay down, until the birds start singing."'

She should get one of the big breweries to release an Amy Winehouse-endorsed Rickstasy. It would sell like hot cakes.

After the disappointment she felt over so many aspects of the album *Frank*, Amy decided to enforce changes for her new venture. 'I didn't want to play the jazz thing up too much again,' she says. 'I was bored of complicated chord structures and needed something more direct. I'd been listening to a lot of girl groups from the fifties and sixties. I liked the simplicity of that stuff. It just gets to the point. So I started thinking about writing songs in that way.'

The differences told in many ways and Amy felt they gave her a more mature edge. 'All the songs I write are about human dynamics, whether it's with girlfriends, boyfriends or family. When I did the last album, *Frank*, I was a very defensive, insecure person, so when I sang about men it was all like, "Fuck you. Who do you think you are?" The new album is more, "I will fight for you; I would do anything for you", or "It's such a shame we couldn't make it work." I feel like I'm not so teenage about relationships.'

It was to be an album made of songs that she would be proud of and would therefore speak more fondly of than she did *Frank*. 'I try to think about things before I say them nowadays,' she confessed. 'I'm a lot less defensive with this record. I'm just so proud of it. I think the record speaks louder than any of my stupid actions or things that I say.'

Whereas *Frank* earned full respect and recognition only some time after its release, *Back to Black* was to be an immediate hit in every sense of the word. Often dark, occasionally despairing but always beautiful and assured, it was an absolute triumph and firmly put Amy on the map of not just those who follow the music business keenly, but everyday folk, too, who simply appreciate a fine tune and a cracking vocal delivery.

It opened with the famous track, 'Rehab'. Blending

traditional soul with a modern twist, 'Rehab' is a joyful, brazen romp of a song that Aretha Franklin would have been proud of. With Mark Ronson at the production controls, the Motown-style horn section builds the drama over the backdrop of bells, handclaps, Wurlitzer organ and piano. It's defiant, brash and unforgivably catchy. Lyrically, it is of course famously about her management team's attempts to make her go into rehabilitation to address her drinking. As for Amy, she'd rather stay at home with her Ray Charles albums. She's convinced she'll be fine, in part because her dad has told her so. 'Rehab' is Amy's most widely recognised song. It has been covered by Girls Aloud, Paolo Nutini, Justin Timberlake and Taking Back Sunday.

Of the song, Amy says, 'I guess when you're quite young and angry at the world, I didn't want to write any songs about love, ever. Then I fell in love and I was like, "Oh, shit!" You know. I used to listen to a lot of stuff like Beastie Boys. I wanted to write loads of tongue-in-cheek songs like that so it was really easy to do something like "Rehab".

The song was written about the time her management tried to get her to check in to the Priory Clinic in Southgate, North London. 'I went in and the guy behind the desk says, "What we do is we're filling out forms." I said, "Oi, listen, don't waste your time." Then he goes, "Why do you think you're here?" and I said, "I don't think I'm an alcoholic, but I'm, you know, depressed. I think it's symptomatic of depression." And he said to me, "Well, I am an alcoholic, I've been here." People who have that kind of rehab mentality, all they wanna do is tell you their story, so you feel better about telling them yours, but you just end up [saying], "Oi, I ain't that bad." '

Next up, the album slows into the sparse, groovy 'You Know I'm No Good'. Blending jazz and R&B, the song is supported by a catchy saxophone line. The lyric concerns Amy's confession of infidelity. However, far from being furious with her for her cheating, when her lover catches her out, he merely shrugs it off. In common with several tracks on her albums, the traditional tune is contrasted by a distinctly modern-day lyric with its mentions of skull T-shirts, chips and pitta. 'You Know…' was used to promote the television show *Mad Men* and as the opening to ITV's *Secret Diary of a Call Girl*. Arctic Monkeys covered it on Jo Wiley's *Live Lounge* on Radio 1.

While 'You Know…' is a little moody and dirty, the doo-wop fun of 'Me and Mr Jones' soon lightens the mood with its sauntering, 1940s feel. Amy bellows out the lyric in a style reminiscent of Dinah Washington. But what are those words about? The Mr Jones of the title is believed to be rapper and Salaam Remi act Nas Jones. The link would seem to be the mention of Destiny, the name of Jones's child with ex-girlfriend Carmen, and of the number 14, because 14 September is the birthday that Winehouse and Nas share. Amy berates him for making her miss a Slick Rick gig. However, she remains in awe of him, her second favourite black Jew after 'Sammy' (presumably Sammy Davis Jr). She might let him make it up to her, she says, and suggests they try again on Saturday.

'A rapper like Nas can tell a story about being in a room, and you feel like you're standing in the corner of that room,' she has explained. 'You know the way it smells, and if someone's smoking.' Her music has the same quality and nowhere is this more true than on 'Me And Mr Jones'.

'Just Friends' maintains the lighter mood. With its gorgeous jazz inflections and Amy's Aretha Franklin-style delivery, it bounces along joyfully. Amy wonders whether she and the man in question can ever be just friends. Although she doesn't resolve the question during the song, and although she is singing of hurt and pain, the music remains upbeat, as does the atmosphere. Which is just as well, as the next song, the titular 'Back to Black', is as dark as they come. Perhaps her most sombre tune, 'Back to Black' is the ultimate heartbreak song and Amy's pain oozes from it like blood. To a doomladen backdrop of reverb guitar, strings and bells, Amy sings of the heartache and despair she feels at the infidelity of her lover. The lyric is almost suicidal, speaking of dying a hundred times and the ultimate low: going back to black.

'There's never a dull moment with Amy... and that includes her album's title track, a gorgeously opulent-but-bitter tale of a tangled love affair gone wrong,' cheered the *Sunday Mirror*, when 'Back to Black' was released as a single. 'It's impossibly smooth and ridiculously good. She is simply on fire on this track,' purred the Scottish *Daily Record*. *Music Week* added that the single is 'a choice cut so soulful you can almost smell the bar-room smoke while listening to it'. The *Financial Times* is a fan of this song, too, one reviewer saying it sounds 'like the sort of brilliantly florid lament that Ennio Morricone used to write for spaghetti westerns'.

Musically, the song has been compared to both 'Baby Love' and 'Jimmy Mack' by Martha Reeves and the Vandellas. The descending melody matches the descending mood of Amy as she deals with her heartbreak and pain. Manchester's *Evening News* described 'Back to Black' on its release as 'one of the best singles of the year'. It's hard to argue. It has been covered by the Rumble Strips and was also sung on *The X Factor* by the hopeful girl band Hope.

If you want a heartbreak song but one that soothes the soul rather than plunges it into deeper agony, then 'Love is a Losing Game' is for you. Again, any sense of redemption is absent from the lyric but it does at least have a calm and resigned feel to it. Musically, a ballad with wonderful strings and a guitar line that has been compared to both the Isley Brothers and Curtis Mayfield, it is like a musical comfort ballad, wrapped round a lovesick soul. Many have commented that 'Love Is...' sounds more like the Amy of the *Frank* era, rather than the Amy of the *Back to Black* days. It has been covered live onstage by Prince. Note, too, the reference to the final frame, no doubt influenced by the many games of pool Amy was playing as she wrote the album. The song was released as a single in December 2007.

Perhaps Amy's most vocally rich song, 'Tears Dry on Their Own' is one of the best-known tracks on the album. It attempts the classic Northern Soul technique of combining a sad theme with a happy, upbeat tune and pulls it off marvellously. Sampling the Motown classic 'Ain't No Mountain High Enough', written by Ashford & Simpson and recorded by Tammi Terrell and Marvin Gaye, and Diana Ross, it is instantly catchy and danceable. Here, Amy is once more heartbroken but she has grown up and toughened up. Therefore, though she cries over the loss, her tears can dry on their own this time.

Ushered in by some choppy chords on a reverb-laden guitar, the dreamy air of 'Wake Up Alone' reflects its lyric, in which Amy describes the aftermath of a break-up. She is staying strong during the day and brings herself up when she finds herself crying. Keeping herself busy, she can stay on top of her emotions while awake. However, it is in her sleep that she has sweat-soaked dreams about him and is, of course, then hurt when she wakes up alone. When she dedicated this song to her imprisoned husband Blake during her winter tour she reduced many audience members to tears, this author included.

A 'Stand By Your Man' for the twenty-first century, 'Some Unholy War' is rarely commented on, which is a shame, because, despite a comparatively uninspiring musical performance, the lyric is inspired and decidedly Amy-esque. She'll stand beside her man whatever fight he is fighting, with her drunken pride and battered guitar case. Her Billie Holiday-style vocals complement the organ and tambourine background neatly. At two minutes and twenty-two seconds, it is the album's shortest tune.

Fans of the Four Tops will have been delighted by 'He Can Only Hold Her'. With nods to James Brown and modern hip hop in its beat, it is a happy tune, certainly when compared with much of the rest of the album. The guitar flows effortlessly and Amy croons over it about the complexities of a particularly tricky relationship. A classic Motown tune, it again deserves a better reputation than it has.

'Addicted' is a wonderfully happy, carefree conclusion to an often dark album. A happy, summery song, it features Amy mischievously singing about a friend's boyfriend who keeps smoking all her weed. Here Amy is sassy, defiant and witty, and the listener can hear the smile on her face as she warns her friend that she won't let her boyfriend back into the house unless he has his own supplies, and that she will be stricter than an airport security team. In the final twist of the album, Amy reveals that weed has done more for her than any dick ever has. Perhaps her happiest ever song, Amy often uses 'Addicted' to kick off her live sets, those familiar opening bass lines setting up many an evening of music and joy.

The response to *Back to Black* was, almost universally, not just positive but absolutely joyously admiring. Indeed, the album surely rates as one of the most consensus-forming releases of recent times. Where the reviews of *Frank* had been largely complimentary, the response to *Back to Black* was almost orgasmic. Helen Brown, writing in the *Daily Telegraph*, said,

Her voice slithers from the soapy-sinuous sound of a woman who can wrap two lovers round her 'likkle' finger, to the heartbroken throaty graze of one left crying on a kitchen floor. Living with raw conviction through the emotional experience of each song on *Back to Black*, Winehouse proves herself a true urban diva.

The *Guardian*'s Dorian Lynskey called it 'a 21st-century soul classic'.

Describing Amy as 'a heavily tattooed, 23-year-old north Londoner with fluctuating weight, a penchant for drink and a vivid sexuality, and a voice that clearly owes a debt to the childhood she spent listening to her daddy's jazz records', the *New Statesman* magazine concluded, '*Back to Black* reveals a darkness that would surely make Winehouse's daddy proud.'

Staying in the liberal press arena, the *Observer* made the track 'Back to Black' its single of the week and, even though reviewer Kitty Empire concluded that the second half of the album is weaker than the first, this matters not, because 'Winehouse could release albums of knuckles cracking from here on in: her reputation is already assured.'

On the BBC website, Matt Harvey covered similar territory: 'The second half of the album isn't quite as good as the first, but that's a minor gripe. One of the best UK albums of the year, with the added advantage that you'll be able to pick it up at the local supermarket checkout...'

Rolling Stone magazine praised Ronson and Remi's assured production, noting that it turns 'classic soul sounds into something big, bright and punchy. The tunes don't always hold up. But the best ones are impossible to dislike.' In *the Evening Standard*, Chris Elwell-Sutton was also praising of the production, gushing, 'To inject so much of her own mixed-up character into such hallowed musical formats was an extraordinary challenge. Luckily, Winehouse has the production, voice and strength of character to pull it off.'

John Lewis, in *Time Out*, said,

It's brilliantly executed by producers Salaam Remi and Mark Ronson, recalling the look-you're-in-the-studio retro soul pastiches of labels like Desco and Daptone. But, crucially, Amy's lyrics (like the lead single 'Rehab', with its splendid assault on therapy culture) retain the contemporary man-baiting obscenities of *Frank*.

In *Attitude*, Jamie Hakim wrote,

An unexpected departure from the jazz stylings of first album *Frank*, Amy comes across like Dinah Washington crossed with 60s girl group the Ronettes. There are also Motown references but overall the sound is darker, the sort of music that delinquents with switchblade scars would drag their backcombed girlfriends across the dancefloor to.

The *Sunday Herald* had this to say: 'Where the original swayed, this one jitters, like a tetchy, frustrated Motown stomper, its urgent drums the perfect backing to the pleading, brash tones of Winehouse, with whom Ronson can seem to do no wrong.'

The Times said, 'This one is tight, packed full of real old-fashioned songs in the manner of soul greats such as Dinah Washington'; and the *Independent* declared, 'For her follow-up to *Frank*, Winehouse has shifted her emphasis from jazz to soulful R&B. It's a measure of her talents that the shift should be so effective.'

Hadley Freeman of the *Guardian* said,

When I interviewed Winehouse in the summer of 2003 she was mouthy, unapologetic and undeniably curvy; by 2005 every tendon in her legs was on show when she was photographed looking lonely and miserable on a night out in London.

So, had Amy reinvented herself deliberately? Music critic Garry Mulholland rejects the notion that the *Back to Black*-era Amy is a wholesale reinvention of the *Frank*-era Amy. 'I accept that she's lost weight,' he says. 'But I don't see it personally as she sat down one day and thought, "I'm going to be thinner and do faux Motown." I see the second album as a continuation and development of the first album. I see her current look as a continuation and development of the look she had a few years ago. She's a proper artist in the way that Bowie and Madonna are. I think every album she makes will have a different sound, and a different look to accompany it. That's what you do, if you're halfway decent. It's just that nowadays we're so unused to halfway decent that people think of it as an extraordinary thing.'

Amy has been compared to many artists, and Jennifer Nine managed an original and novel comparison in her review of the album on *Yahoo Music*. She said the album's

fearless knack, along with the ability to get into the very soul of much-aped but rarely matched pop genres, hasn't been done this well since Elvis Costello was in his savage prime. And frankly, when you factor in the knock-'em-dead voice and the killer eyeliner, Elvis is nowhere f*cking close.

On the webzine *PopMatters*, the reviewer said, '*Back to Black* finds a fearless artist saying whatever she damn well pleases. And we best listen up.' Even the posh old *Financial Times* chimed in, asking in a quiz, 'Which colour does Amy Winehouse return to, according to her current bestselling CD?'

Amy has discussed the inspiration behind the album's songs. 'So, "Rehab" is the first single from the album. It's all about my revolving door rehab experience. I said no! "You Know I'm No Good" is about how I couldn't be faithful, and the title comes from my defensiveness when I got found out. Which leads us to "Back to Black", the title track. I split up with my boyfriend and had a few black months. Say no more!

"Me & Mr Jones"? Well... I didn't mind when my ex didn't get me into the Slick Rick show, but Nas? Nobody stands in between me and my man! "Tears Dry on Their Own" comes from when I was in a relationship that I knew was doomed, but that I wouldn't be too devastated when it ended…Sometimes you just need to find time in the day to have fun, not sex. That's what "Just Friends" is about.

'But you know when you're in a failing relationship and you're trying to make it work? Well that's "Love is a Losing Game" – how hopeless and desolate you can feel. Finally, there's "Addicted". Now, my best friend can smoke however much of mine she likes, but her boyfriend? That shit don't fly!'

Paolo Hewitt is a renowned music writer and is the author of respected works on everyone from Steve Marriott of the Small Faces to Oasis and Paul Weller. In an interview with the author, he expanded on why Amy had such a success with *Back to Black*. 'She does what all the greats do,' he said. 'She takes from various sources and then makes it her own. People are very lazy when it comes to black music. They would never ever call the Smiths a prog-rock band but they feel like they can write about "the Amy Winehouse-influenced Motown album". There's so much more than just Motown going on there. For me, when I heard "Rehab", I just heard fifties and sixties New Orleans music. There's so much there: jazz, R&B and more.

'When I hear one of her tunes that I've not heard before on the radio, I always think, "Wow, what is this?" It's always her that makes me sit up and take notice. She always brings something new to the table, twists it round and makes it her own. Part of that is to do with her voice but she's also a very creative artist. She really knows what makes music work and makes her own music work the same way.

'The only problem with her is she's far too much into the Billie Holiday, broken woman in the bar at two in the morning with a bottle of whisky, singing about her man leaving her. I think she's too in love with that. It gets a bit samey, but that's a minor quibble.'

Some have wondered whether the great form that Amy found herself in whenever she worked with producer Mark

Ronson might have been motivated by some romantic sparks between the pair. 'It's the most ridiculous thing I've ever heard,' he laughed. 'She calls me the big sister she never had! Amy makes a really nice meatball dinner. She's good at making Jewish-mother food.' Amy always says, "Don't ask me about anything new" because she just likes what she likes,' he says, 'so I just let her find a song. As soon as she started singing "Valerie" I knew she'd sung it in the shower a few times.'

Nonetheless, Ronson was clearly an influential man in her success. As was Raye Cosbert. According to EMI's Guy Moot, 'There are two pivotal moments in Amy's career: the introduction of Mark Ronson and of Raye.' Raye Cosbert had promoted her concerts since 2003, and, when she left Brilliant 19, it was to him she turned. 'We had a chance meeting one day in Camden,' Cosbert recalls. 'She told me about her situation, said she'd heard that I was doing the odd thing management-wise and we just hit it off from there really.'

Cosbert had previously worked with the likes of Blur, Robbie Williams, Lily Allen, Massive Attack, Björk and Public Enemy. Guy Moot says of Cosbert, 'He is incredibly calm and, by remaining calm, he focuses on what the goals are and at the same time harnesses the more erratic artistic moments that Amy has.'

Moot is particularly positive about the effect that Cosbert's full management has had on Amy's live performances. 'He is incredibly experienced in the live arena, so the production and the presentation has improved dramatically,' says Moot. 'It was incredibly hit-and-miss before: you really didn't know whether it was going to be a good show or not. She is an incredible live performer now.'

On the success of *Back to Black*, Cosbert is hugely positive and proud. Asked how many copies the album can go on to sell, he replied, 'How long is a piece of string? Let me put it this way, all the predictions we had initially are now out the window because of the success of the record. We all had different views of what we thought the album would achieve commercially and we've exceeded them all.'

Chapter Six

BEAT IT!

In October 2006, Amy Winehouse was booked to appear on *The Charlotte Church Show*. It proved to be a memorable performance. Church's show had begun broadcasting the previous month and was a huge step forward for the Welsh singer, who had already appeared as both a guest and as a guest-host on *Have I Got News For You*. Her new show was a mixture of studio guests, comedy sketches and musical performances. It was here that Amy came in, of course.

Amy and Church had agreed to perform a duet of 'Beat It' by Michael Jackson at the end of the show. However, it soon became clear that Amy was not in an ideal state to perform. Rumours have it that, on the day, Amy had downed champagne for breakfast and killer cocktails for lunch. 'When she turned up for rehearsal she was drunk, she kept forgetting her words,' remembers Church. 'Come the show, we had to do a few takes.' One wonders what the rejected takes sounded like because the one that was broadcast was fairly chaotic itself.

Amy leads in with the first line but her performance is slurred and she seems to be struggling to remember the words. Church then sings her line but is clearly watching Amy like a hawk, with an expression somewhere between concern and distaste. Each time she handed back to Amy, Church had a secret signal. 'Amy kept forgetting the words. I told her when I squeeze you it's your turn to sing,' she says. 'We did it with me poking her in the back.'

As they join together to sing the first chorus, Amy's body language is somewhat sheepish. The start of the second verse sees Amy seeming more energetic and focused, but then, as Church takes over, she pointedly sings the line 'You're playing with your life' directly at Amy. As if in response, Amy makes a mess of the second verse's final line. The rest of the song passes without incident but any rapport between the two singers has long since passed. They do, however, manage to embrace each other at the end of the performance. Amy looks little short of relieved that the ordeal is over.

Church's decision to take the moral high ground over Amy after the show was somewhat hypocritical. She has long spoken of her own partying ways, boasting, 'I can sink 'em.' She adds, 'If I'm home, I'll start with a Cheeky Vimto – double port and a bottle of WKD Blue in the same glass. It tastes just like Vimto or Ribena. They're lethal. Once I'm out, I'll have about ten double vodkas. Then I'm pretty much KO'd.'

She celebrated her nineteenth birthday in February with a seventy-two-hour bender and has been photographed looking the worse for wear. To be fair to Church, she did later say, 'From the last series I enjoyed everyone that came on, really. Amy Winehouse was wild, very different and really nice. She was lovely, a little sweetheart.'

Furthermore, given Amy's reputation at this point in her career, to invite her onto a chat show, sit her in a green room when such places are famed for having free wine on tap, and then make her wait until the end of the show to perform would seem to be a recipe for trouble. Equally, the song 'Beat It' seemed a peculiar choice for Amy to sing in any state, since it didn't play to many of her plentiful qualities. Could it be that this was a deliberate attempt to stir up controversy and therefore add to the 1.9 million viewers who were watching the show?

If so, it worked. The *Mirror* ran the story big, under the headline AMY WINO! EXCLUSIVE: SINGER DRUNK FOR CHARLOTTE CHURCH TV CHAT. The *Daily Telegraph* added that Amy was 'outrageous, but out of this world', and millions more have by now watched the footage of her performance on the Internet, where it has become a hit. Many chat and light-entertainment shows have benefited from having a controversial or drunken appearance. From Oliver Reed to George Best and Tara Palmer-Tomkinson, it's a well-trodden path. Indeed, such is the competition in today's television world that it could be argued that such shows have no hope of succeeding without such an incident.

As well as criticising Amy's performance on the night, Church also got stuck into her about her cancellation of her US tour. She said, 'It's rude if you ask me. I always turned up and did my duties.' When confronted with these remarks, Amy snapped, 'Church is an arrogant cow. And Bono isn't much better. He thinks he's God.' Of her appearance on the show, she said, 'I was drunk. Charlotte invited me on the show, so she must know I'm a bit of a liability.'

Amy was not the only person to put in a tipsy and controversial appearance on *The Charlotte Church Show*. In the same series, comedian Johnny Vegas sank bitter and cocktails, leched over female guests and turned the interview into an absurdity. An audience member said, 'It was like watching a car crash. Johnny was off his face and took every opportunity to wind her up – she didn't have the experience to keep him under control.' At one point, Church reminded Vegas that they had performed karaoke at her mother's hotel the previous year and Vegas replied, 'Yes, and I shagged your grandma too.' He also had a pop at his host's music, saying, 'I listened to your album and it was shit.' Losing her patience, Church snapped and shouted, 'Shut the fuck up,' and slapped the comic.

Not that all this controversy did Church much harm. She was soon picking up awards, including Best Female Comedy Newcomer at the British Comedy Awards and Funniest TV Personality at the *Loaded* magazine LAFTA awards. She also got the series recommissioned by Channel 4. Andrew Newman, head of entertainment and comedy at Channel 4, said, 'Charlotte has proved herself to be a hugely talented star and has got better and better each week.' Maybe Charlotte owes Amy one.

While Amy had made many laugh with her performance on *The Charlotte Church Show*, she had people in stitches of laughter on BBC panel show *Never Mind the Buzzcocks*. Her first appearance on the show came in March 2004. Memorable moments included when Phill Jupitus recounted some rumours about Lou Reed and Amy let out a rising whistle, which prompted general laughter. 'It's my Jewish-mother cluck noise,' she explained. The show's then host, Mark Lamarr, quipped that she sounded like a cheap firework. During the intros round – which was adapted for this edition so the contestants hummed the instrumental break, rather than the intro, for each song – she was described by Jupitus as sounding like an angry kitten. 'It's because I'm small,' she protested. 'I can't manipulate my voice like a big man like you can.'

Having been compared to a firework and kitten, she was then asked if she was 'a cockney rabbi'. Then there was just time for her song 'Stronger Than Me' to form a part of the final lyrics round, for Lamarr to mention her childhood band Sweet 'n' Sour and then the show was over. A fairly typical *Buzzcocks* edition, but one that scarcely hinted at the entertainment to come during her second appearance on the show, which came in November 2006.

Lining up alongside GMTV presenter Penny Smith, Alex Pennie and Andrew Maxwell, Amy put in an absolutely majestic performance, utterly outwitting the show's new sharp host Simon Amstell and turning regular guest Bill Bailey into an irrelevance. When Amstell introduced Amy, he quipped, 'Amy's likes include Kelly Osbourne and the smell of petrol. I quite like matches, let's do lunch.' He also said to her, 'It's lovely to have you here. Part of the BBC's new remit: more Jews, less carbon emissions.'

GMTV presenter Smith – who, incidentally, was wearing a top that looked like a plate of hummus with cumin and paprika sprinkled over it – asked, 'Amy, is that hair yours, and is anything living in it?' Amstell interrupted to gasp, 'That's not the GMTV way!' then Amy answered, 'Oh, yeah it's all mine, 'cos I bought it.' Soon after this, Amy revealed that later that evening she was due to meet Pete Doherty to record a song. Amstell shrieked, 'Don't go near him! Do something with Katie Melua. There you are.' Amy sank back in her seat and said, 'I'd rather have cat-AIDS, thank you.'

Amy's Melua quip grabbed the loudest laugh of the night so far but host Amstell soon regained the upper hand when Amy told him that her 'new thing' was making a noise that sounded like 'psht, psht'. 'Is it?' Amstell responded. 'I thought it was crack.' Amy turned to him and asked scornfully, 'Do I look like Russell Brand?' Amstell jumped straight in and said, 'Uh, yes.' (Incidentally, Brand once wrote, 'Amy Winehouse had bigger hair than me. She says she uses polystyrene cement. Must get some.')

Other classic one-liners from Amy on the night included (on Ben Elton), 'I don't think there's such a thing as integrity or being a sell-out, I just think he's a wanker.' When Amstell said how much he preferred the younger Amy, who had appeared on his Channel 4 *Popworld* show, she said, 'We were close,' and then, running her palm down his face, added, 'Now she's dead.'

She then turned and spat over her shoulder. 'I will wipe it up,' she pleaded. 'I just didn't want to gurgle.' Amstell said, 'This is not a football match. You come here, full of... crack... spitting all over things.' Amy sighed, 'Let it die, please. Let it die.' Amstell responded, 'The addiction I'd like to die... this isn't even a pop quiz any more: it's an intervention, Amy.' During the closing round, Amstell asked where the following lyric came from: 'They tried to make me go to rehab...' Amy jumped in with, 'I said no, no, no.' Amstell told her, 'Correct. In hindsight... I think maybe "yes", maybe...' Amy – who said on her *I Told You I Was Trouble* DVD that she loves Amstell – took it in good spirit.

Amy's performance was much discussed that week and has since become a huge hit on YouTube. One user of that website, called Stuart, even filmed his own video in response to it. 'I saw her the other day on *Buzzcocks*', he says. 'What happened? She looks like a train wreck!'

Before long, *Buzzcocks* would become mired in controversy when Ordinary Boys singer Preston stormed out in disgust after Amstell made some disparaging remarks about his wife Chantelle. Donny Tourette attempted to replicate Amy's wit when he appeared on the show but was eaten alive by Amstell's and Bailey's wit.

Looking back on her entertaining television spots, Amy is

AMY WINEHOUSE

characteristically unrepentant. 'No, it doesn't really bother me,' she sneers. 'There have been times when I've done stuff on telly and I've been drunk because I was bored. Why not be drunk? The thing is I'm not trying to protect "Winehouse, the Brand", know what I mean? I don't look at things in a long-term way. I've got a long time between sound check and the actual show so fuck it, I'll get drunk.

'Apparently, the other night at a gig, some girl came up to me afterwards and she goes "Hello" and gave me a kiss on the cheek, and as she went away she goes to my boyfriend, "God, she's fucked, isn't she?" and I just saw red and smacked her. I don't remember this at all. Then I took my boyfriend home and started beating him up.'

At a concert in Brighton, between songs, Amy once asked the audience where the best venue for a post-gig game of pool could be found in the seaside town. She had previously rated a concert at Glasgow's King Tut's club as one of her best, purely for the availability of a pool table, which almost got her into trouble.

'That was a great gig for me... It was brilliant. I really, really like that place. There aren't that many venues that have a pool table downstairs, you know. I put money on the side of the table and came back for my game, and these guys were playing. I was like, "Oi, I put my coin down," and they were like, "No, you didn't." I took off before someone hit me with a pool cue.'

On 6 January 2007, Amy was booked to perform at G-A-Y, the gay night at London's Astoria venue at 157 Charing Cross Road. There is a companion bar a mere mince away on the famous Old Compton Street. The club, hosted by Jeremy Joseph, is perhaps the UK's leading gay night. Attracting a poppy, youthful crowd, it has been the venue for numerous big-name musicians down the years. Kylie Minogue has performed there, as have Westlife, Donna Summer, the Spice Girls and Boyzone. Such appearances often capture the imagination of the media, whether it is reports of teenage girls who are heartbroken to learn that their pin-ups are playing to a gay crowd, or McFly's always memorable performances there, which have seen them both strip and set their own pubic hair alight. Indeed, if you want to get a gay following and create a stir in the press, you could do a lot worse than book yourself in at G-A-Y.

For weeks, the venue had been trumpeting Amy's forthcoming appearance with the slogan, TRY TO MAKE ME GO TO REHAB/I SAY NO, NO, NO... TRY TO MAKE ME GO TO G-A-Y/I SAY YES, YES, YES. Given Amy's huge popularity in the gay community, the night seemed set to become an absolute triumph and tickets for the night were quickly snapped up by excited fans. This disproved the whispers in some circles that Amy either was – or was perceived by some gay men to be – homophobic. The rumour sprang from the line in 'Stronger Than Me' when Amy asks her weakling boyfriend if he is gay. The truth, as we have seen, is that Amy meant no offence to any gay man with this line and none was taken in any serious quarter. In the event, while Amy did not in fairness set light to her pubic hair, nor strip naked, she managed to capture the following day's headlines in her own way.

One person present described Amy as looking 'a little unsteady on her feet' and 'smelling of booze' when she arrived at the venue at around midnight. At 1.30 a.m., club host Jeremy Joseph strode onto the stage and warmly introduced Amy to the cheering masses. After a brief delay, she took to the stage and was greeted by a deafening welcome. The band launched into 'Back to Black' and all seemed well for a while.

Then Amy started repeatedly holding her stomach and grimacing with discomfort. She also appeared to belch or heave a couple of times, holding her hand to her mouth and looking a little wobbly. By the time it came to the final chorus of the opening track, she was interrupting her own vocals and seemed extremely disoriented. Before the song even finished, she rushed from the stage holding her stomach. Joseph quickly replaced her on the stage and told the confused audience that Amy was vomiting and asked them to bear with her. 'But she never came back. Everyone was booing,' said one audience member. Eventually, news came through that she was not returning to the stage and heckles joined in with the boos. Some audience members stamped their feet.

The story was quickly put out by Amy's people that her ill health was not alcohol-related but was actually the result of food poisoning. She told a journalist the following morning as she nursed a smoothie, 'I haven't had a drink in a few days.' Not that many folk were in a mood to believe this story. As journalist Kitty Empire quipped in the *Guardian*, 'The nation's water coolers, Soho pubs, message boards and gossip websites rattled with a collective snort of derision.' Instead, many preferred to believe the other explanation doing the rounds: that Amy had spent the day drinking heavily with Kelly Osbourne. The pair have certainly been known to enjoy sinking a few glasses together. Osbourne said, 'You should watch out. We call ourselves Team Evil. We like to go around causing trouble.' IT'S BARF TIME FOR AMY, ran the *Sun* headline. It certainly had not been Amy's finest hour.

The following month, she was able to atone for her first G-A-Y appearance when she was booked to return to the Astoria for an appearance under the *NME* banner. During the *NME* performance, while trying to locate Mitch in the crowd, she suddenly realised she had been singing towards the wrong man. 'You're impersonating my dad! I've been singing to you all night,' she laughed. Particular highlights on the night were 'Love is a Losing Game', 'You Know I'm No Good' and 'Back to Black'. However, the one-hour set was brought to a punctual end because, following the concert, the venue was turning into another G-A-Y night at which Amy was due to perform, to make up for her premature exit in January. 'I'm surprised they let me in,' she quipped with a hearty chuckle. 'I thought there would be crowds of angry homosexuals at the door, waiting to batter me! I know I look as though I can handle myself, but...'

By the time she bounced back on the stage in front of the G-A-Y crowd, Amy was ready to prove her doubters wrong and was suitably sheepish and repentant when she told the crowd, 'Thank you so much for coming. I can't believe you had me back.'

They had her back again, in April, when, wearing a white vest and appearing particularly lucid, she gave a fantastic performance and once more won the audience over. At the end of the performance, host Jeremy Joseph offered her the choice of a bunch of flowers or a bottle of champagne. She quipped, 'I don't drink.'

News then broke that Amy had been shortlisted in two categories for the forthcoming BRIT awards. How far she had come since her days at the BRIT Performing Arts & Technology School in Croydon, which was funded by the body that ran the BRITs. 'Amy is really pleased to be shortlisted and honoured that some are tipping her to win,' said a spokesperson, adding cheekily, 'She'll probably go out now and have a pint or two to celebrate.' Amy's first words on the matter were typically down-to-earth. 'There's going to be all these really cool people at the BRITs show, but me and my dad will be looking for the Terry Wogans and Fern Brittons,' she smiled.

On the night, she arrived at the awards wearing a yellow dress. However, once it became time for her performance, she had changed into a fetching red number. She gave a faultless performance of 'Rehab'. The worst the critics could say the following day was to express their disappointment that she wasn't drunk or chaotic at all. The evening kicked off with a fantastic performance of 'I Don't Feel Like Dancing' by the Scissor Sisters. Ten garishly dressed dancers bopped behind the band and before long the venue was warmed up, with even some of the stiff suits letting themselves go.

Russell Brand was the compere for the evening and he kicked off the proceedings with a joke that the stage set 'looked not unlike an Amy Winehouse tattoo', a quip that he later credited to Oasis guitarist and songwriter Noel Gallagher. When it came to introducing Amy, he said she was 'a woman whose surname sounds increasingly like the state of her liver'. He added that her acceptance speech could 'easily have come from a London cabbie'.

She had walked a little unsteadily to the stage and said in her distinctive cockney twang, 'Thank you very much. I'm glad my mum and dad are here, to be honest.' Later on, looking back at the night Amy was more loquacious, saying, 'I was flattered to even be nominated, let alone win. It was very exciting, actually. I hadn't seen my mum in ages, so it was nice to see my mum. My dad was pissed. My dad was so funny. It was a good night, I really enjoyed it.'

Amy got fantastic reviews for her performance of 'Rehab' on the night and also for what she and Lily Allen wore to the event. 'Amy, Lily and the rest of the Brit pack staged a spectacular fashion show on the biggest night of the pop music calendar,' said the *Daily Mail*.

Speaking of Allen, there were reports that she and Amy had a huge row on the evening of the ceremony. Allen had been up for a number of awards but ended up winning none of them. According to an eyewitness at Heathrow airport, she admitted, 'I had a real slanging match with Amy Winehouse. We had a really bad row. It was terrible. I'm miserable and don't want to talk about it.' An onlooker at the airport added that Lily waited alone for a flight to Washington, DC: 'She had tears streaming down her face and she seemed as though she hadn't slept a wink. She looked really rough and hung over. Someone asked if she was all right and she said she'd had a bust-up with Amy Winehouse. She was sniffing and wiping tears from her cheeks. She looked like a little lost schoolgirl.'

However spokespeople for both women denied the incident. A representative for Allen said, 'I don't know anything about an argument. As far as I know they've always got on OK.' Amy's camp added, 'Lily was crying because she was tired and emotional after her big night. They didn't have an argument – they're friends.' Allen herself added, 'The story about me being in tears either because I didn't win a BRIT or had a fight with Amy is complete rubbish. She and I are friends and we were hanging out at the BRITs and at the Oasis party afterwards. I was talking to her for ages. I always said that I wasn't expecting to win, and that if I wasn't going to win then I hoped Amy did. I'm very pleased for her.

'The pictures of me crying in the papers were taken when I was saying goodbye to my boyfriend, who I haven't seen much of recently. I've been working really hard and travelling a lot and I only got to see him at the BRITs, so the tears were just because I was leaving to get on yet another plane.'

Reports vary as to just how hard Amy's celebrations after the ceremony were. The *Daily Star* said, 'Winehouse claimed she would party all night, but she was later seen walking around the Mocoto bar and the Cuckoo Club looking seriously sober, saying she just wanted to celebrate with family and friends.' However, Mark Ronson says that he and Amy partied hard after the BRITs. 'We got wasted together after the BRITs and I passed out on her floor hugging an animal rug at 7 a.m.,' he recalls.

The final word on the night goes to Amy, who managed to take the time to offer her sympathy to Robbie Williams, who had recently gone into a clinic to address his demons. 'I feel gutted for him. Addiction to prescription drugs is a really hard thing. I hope he comes out OK,' she said. The following day she and a companion were spotted out and about. One onlooker said, 'They kept their heads down and didn't say too much. It must have been a very good time the previous night.'

HMV's Gennaro Castaldo puts into perspective what a BRIT triumph meant for Amy's career: 'Aside from the kudos that it gives you, winning a BRIT or performing at the awards ceremony can seriously enhance an artist's recording career. The profile that it gives you means that successful artists can break out of their immediate fan base to connect with a much wider audience. This is happening right now to Amy Winehouse.

'It will help take her to that next level of stardom, as we have seen in the past with the likes of Robbie Williams and Coldplay.'

Back to Black, which had slipped to Number 5, went to Number 2 in the wake of the BRITs, with sales up nearly 200 per cent at HMV, and downloads of her single 'Rehab' shot up 40 per cent during the show itself.

Within months came Amy's performance at the Glastonbury Festival. Although she began the set nervously, it proved to be a memorable and enjoyable performance. Sauntering onto the Pyramid Stage just after 3 p.m., Amy expressed her gratitude that fans were willing to stand in the rain to listen to her sing.

She was utterly entertaining: swinging her hips seductively, singing her heart out and even muttering to herself and giggling at times. It made for quite a spectacle.

Then the bizarre: someone flew over the crowd in a paraglider. Soon after this the rain packed it in and was replaced by the sun. The track which heralded this dramatic brightening of the conditions? *Back to Black*, what else? Before long a beautiful rainbow framed the stage, and Amy jubilantly reminded the audience that she had promised them sun and delivered them the sun. Rosie Swash said of Amy's performance that 'she bares more than a passing resemblance to a rabbit caught in the headlights... she never quite loses the slightly traumatised expression'. Another observer described Amy as resembling 'an extra from *Star Trek*'. What concert where they at?

She also appeared at the Isle of Wight festival that summer. Wearing a vest and shortcut jeans, she gave an extraordinarily accomplished performance. The *Spectator* review seemed to be of another concert:

It was like seeing Bambi bounce into a clearing to find himself faced with a firing squad. Terrified, she fidgeted and scampered on the spot, calming down only when she sang, and it looked as if it took every ounce of muscle and morphine she could muster not to run for the hills.

Later in the festival, when the veteran rockers the Rolling Stones took to the stage, Amy joined them to duet with Mick

Jagger on the Motown classic 'Ain't Too Proud to Beg'. This 1966 hit for the Temptations has also been covered by Rick Astley, Willie Bobo, Count Basie and his Orchestra, JJ Jackson, the J Evans Band, Ben Harper and others. Amy and Jagger were perfect together. It was a great performance all round by Amy and one she enjoyed, even if she almost missed it.

'I'm not very ambitious at all,' she said soon after the show. 'I almost didn't come to this concert. I almost didn't go to the gig in Sweden yesterday. I almost didn't go to the Isle of Wight, I almost didn't do it.' Citing Blake's worries as the reason for her near-misses, she added, 'I just want him to be happy. And, if for some reason he's unhappy, then it just floors me.'

These words scarcely did justice to the drama and controversy that Amy and Blake's relationship was to cause in the coming months.

Chapter Seven

A CIVIL PARTNERSHIP?

One day, while talking to friends, Blake Fielder-Civil received a text message on his mobile phone from Kelly Osbourne. The text informed him that Amy was in a hotel room in Los Angeles, wearing *his* underpants. As strange moments in his relationship went, this was small fry. Their relationship has been utterly wild. It's been described as everything from a modern-day Sid Vicious and Nancy Spungen, to a dangerous, *Fatal Attraction*-style pairing.

Blake met Amy in 2005. He recalls, 'We met at a pub called the Good Mixer in Camden. I'd just had a good win at the bookies so I went to the pub to celebrate, opened the door and Amy was the first person I saw and that was it. The drinks were on me for the first and last time! And from that night onwards, we began our tortuous love affair.

'When we met we were attracted to each other instantly and

we've never stopped being that way,' he said of their love-at-first-sight encounter. 'I know me and Amy are going to be together. She's the love of my life.' Within a month, that love was expressed in artistic form, as Amy got a new tattoo. Inked on her chest, over her heart, is a button pocket with the word 'Blake's' on it. Hence, she was expressing that he'll always be close to her heart. Blake, too, loves tattoos and even has the word 'Sailor' inked on the inside of his lip.

However, this initial courtship was not to last long because Blake already had a girlfriend. How inconvenient! As we were subsequently to hear in one of Amy's best-loved songs, Blake quickly went back to his girlfriend and Amy, well, she went back to black. To deal with her heartache, Amy quickly took up with a new man, Alex Claire. Claire was twenty-one when he met Amy and was quickly taken in by her 'very striking face with big brown eyes that suck you in'.

As for Amy, she recalls, 'I made him buy me a tequila because they were refusing to serve me on account of a golf-ball-sized lump on my head from the previous night. A few drinks later I was sat on his lap.'

The venue for this tequila moment was the Hawley Arms in Camden. Within eight weeks, chef and musician Claire had moved in with her. Claire has spoken of their wild sex romp. They were once almost thrown out of a cinema in north London as their passionate clinch became more and more passionate. Presumably *V For Vendetta* hadn't grabbed their attention, then. They also had sex backstage at a concert in Southampton, minutes before Amy strolled onto the stage.

In his torrid kiss-and-tell interview with the *News of the World*, entitled BONDAGE, BEATINGS AND BITINGS, Claire claimed that Amy 'loved being dominated as well as dominating'. He said she once pushed his head under the bathwater during sex. 'I was under for several seconds. I couldn't breathe and started freaking out.' Then there was the time he was 'clobbered by her huge beehive during a romp'. Never a dull moment, then!

During their year-long affair, they split three times but each time they would get back together after making up. However, the main issue facing their relationship was Blake. Claire found it hard to believe that Amy and Blake really were history. She would promise to have her 'Blake's' tattoo removed but then, hours later, would be spotted not having it removed but hanging out with her former lover. One night, in March 2007, she was spotted enjoying a passionate moment with both Claire and Blake in one single night. Confusion reigned not just in Claire's mind but in the minds of Amy's friends, too. 'I saw Amy when she was on *The Sharon Osbourne Show* back in October 2006,' says one friend. 'She had Blake with her. All the time she was talking about her "boyfriend" – Alex – but was sitting on Blake's lap and snogging him. She was saying, "Read me out those text messages I sent you – the filthy ones." It was all pretty gross.'

Later on, Amy and Blake confirmed that many of these suspicions were justified. 'Our relationship never really stopped, did it, babe?' said Blake. 'I was sneaking around making phone calls and we'd meet up for five minutes or ten minutes and in the end we just couldn't carry on doing that.'

'Yes,' replied Amy. 'There was a time when we didn't talk to each other but that was because we realised it was better not to talk than talk and cause irreparable damage.'

Amy said of Blake, 'I'm still really close to him as a friend – though Alex doesn't like me seeing him, which is understandable.' By this time, she had written 'Back to Black', about her initial break-up with Blake, and was surprised that the theme of the song didn't cause more of an issue with Claire, who was instead a big fan of the song. 'I told him the song was about Blake but he didn't care. Weird, I know!'

So, few were surprised when Amy returned to Blake. However, while Claire may not have been surprised, he was heartbroken, as he revealed in a dramatic outburst on his MySpace page:

> After turning up at three in the morning at The Hawley Arms, I saw the ex with her ex and I saw red mist. I was shaking like a leaf and decided to get... leathered while she sat there inebriated and on the lap of her ex. [I'm] skint, heartbroken and homeless – bad luck comes in threes as the old saying goes, but s**t, what's a man to do?

His outburst – slammed as 'pathetic' by one of the tabloids – continued, 'A friend gave me a little something I hadn't had in a while – MDMA. I always forget how enjoyable everything was after you taste that rank shit, especially with a couple of Valium, three lines and a little dark rum to wash it down.' Amy says she understands why Claire felt hurt but adds, 'Something tells me he'll be all right.'

Her father Mitch said that Amy's busy schedule caused problems with her relationship with Claire. 'It's like she cut out my heart, bit a chunk out of it, threw it on the floor and stomped all over it,' said Claire. 'She's scared to be happy. I hope she finds happiness one day. She needs looking after but I'm glad that's not my responsibility any more.'

Amy's relationship with Claire might have seemed eccentric but her tryst with Blake was to prove spectacularly unconventional, wild, controversial and newsworthy. Upon hooking up with him for a second time, Amy declared, 'He's the one.' But who was he? Having been described as everything from a 'rock' for Amy, to an evil man, the source of all her woes, where did this young man appear from?

There were a few hints of the drama to come when Blake was a fresh-faced pupil at the strict Bourne Grammar School in Lincolnshire. 'He was a bit geeky, to be honest,' says one former classmate. 'He wasn't really interested in working hard but he seemed to have lots of mates and was fairly popular with the girls.' Another fellow pupil, Mark Stoker, said, 'Blake was cheeky and cocky but not enough to get into trouble. He wasn't thick but just didn't have the application to work. When he left school he moved down to London and we lost touch.' Having tracked Blake's infamous life since, Stoker reflects, 'He has obviously been influenced by the music scene. He certainly never dressed like he does now when we were at school.'

Blake was, however, showing some interest in style while at school. He took an interest in hairdressing – no doubt attracting a few jibes from his fellow male pupils – and photographs of him at school reveal he had an angelic, floppy centre-parting style. His creative side also stretched to his devouring literature and dreaming of becoming a journalist. After school, he set off for the bright lights of the capital city and sent a dispatch of his glamorous new lifestyle back to his former schoolmates via the nostalgic Friends Reunited website. 'Live in London innit,' he wrote on his online profile. 'Cut hair for fashion shoots, go out in town and enjoy my girlfriend lots. Academia never my forte but taking a fashion design degree at Chelsea this year and a ND in history of art. Would quite like to hear from some people and I hope I do.'

However, Blake did not need to rely on old friends from school because he had a new set of pals in the capital. One, who used to go clubbing frequently with Blake says, 'He's kind of a charming bad boy. He's the sort of bloke who's got all the chat – who's got a little twinkle in his eye. He'll go out and misbehave and do who knows what, but he'd never let a woman go through a door second. He's always called a "music video assistant", or a "gopher" but I don't know about that. I don't know where he gets his money from.'

He's said to have had a number of jobs in shops and bars in north London. It was of course in a bar that he first met Amy, who was said to have been drawn to him 'as a moth to a flame', attracted to 'a bit of rough'. Then came the tattoo on her chest, and, by the time she was reunited with him following her split with Claire, it looked as if the relationship was finally living up to the serious billing it received when the pair had first met. She and Blake seemed inseparable. 'It's like they can't live without each other,' said one friend. At the time, this seemed a beautiful expression of the romantic depth of the couple's bond. It would soon take on a whole new and sinister resonance.

The first thing that Blake had to adapt to once he started dating Amy was the glare of publicity. Amy admits that he found it a challenge. 'There's no point in being pissed off about things you can't control. It's cool. It causes problems with my husband, though. He doesn't like it,' she has said since her marriage to Blake in May 2007. The most visible and brutal expression of this came in the shape of the paparazzi, who would follow the couple around. 'I'm protective of Amy as any man would be of his wife,' he has said. 'It's natural. To have a scrum of photographers shouting, thrusting cameras and flashing them in your face can be quite intimidating but Amy seems to have accepted this is the way her life is going to be from now on.'

Amy agrees: 'Yes, you're right, it can be intimidating. And it can be scary sometimes when people I don't know seem to know me, but that's about it really.'

Many celebrities have found that they have lost otherwise promising relationships because their non-famous partners have found living in the public eye was too much to take. It is to Blake's enormous credit and a hugely positive sign of the couple's prospects of future happiness that he has striven hard to come to terms with the pressures of Amy's fame.

Amy admits that she is a high-maintenance girlfriend to have, 'in that I expect my boyfriend to come to my house and sleep with me every night. I'm an all-or-nothing person, but I also like to look after my man and make him feel like a king.' Prior to meeting Blake, she had spoken of the difficulty of balancing her career and a boyfriend. 'At the moment I don't have the time to be able to respect a boyfriend properly, and I can't expect a boyfriend to respect and honour what I do right now, so I am not looking for anything on a surface level.'

Amy and Blake went out for one of their typical nights on the tiles in April 2007. Drinks were enjoyed; laughter, chat and much more besides were shared. Then, when they got home, Blake turned to Amy and asked her to marry him. He didn't get an instant answer, as Amy revealed: 'I took a day to finally agree.' Not that she was in two minds. 'I am so pleased Blake proposed. It's fucking amazing, fantastic,' she beamed, flashing her £3,000 Tiffany engagement ring to her friends. Speaking to reporters on the steps outside a Camden pub, Amy said, 'I'm a very lucky girl to have found someone I love so much. I hope to be with him for the rest of my life. We haven't set a date yet or anything like that. Obviously, we're both young and it's frightening. But it's the right thing to do. That's why I agreed.'

Soon the plans for the wedding were under way – as was the inevitable press speculation. One report claimed that Amy was demanding that her fiancé convert to Judaism in order to marry her. 'He isn't religious so it's no skin off his nose,' said a source. 'He will do anything she wants and has spoken to her dad about it.' However, one eyewitness on the day of their wedding on 18 May suggests he wouldn't do anything Amy wants, at all. As he strutted down the hotel corridor, he was said to be singing to himself, 'They tried to make me sign a prenup but I said no, no, no.'

The hotel in question was the Shore Club Hotel in Miami, where Amy and Blake booked a £2,500-a-night room for their wedding trip. While there, they certainly celebrated in style. It is estimated that they spent £1,000 on room service, including countless bottles of Veuve Clicquot champagne at £90 a time. They even had the in-house masseur visit them.

'Amy told Blake that she'd spare no expense – she's working so hard now that they tried to cram two weeks' worth of fun into two days,' said a friend. 'They locked themselves in and wouldn't even leave to let the chambermaids change the linen! Every few hours, they'd call and ask for bubbly and occasionally French fries. They seemed far more interested in booze than food!' It is estimated that the bill for their stay eventually came to £9,000 all in.

The events of the day of the wedding are still somewhat mysterious. It is known, though, that Amy wore a short floral-patterned sundress and Blake wore a retro grey suit for the brief ceremony at the Miami-Dade County Marriage License Bureau in Florida. Marriage clerk Sammy Calixte, who conducted the ceremony, said, 'They came in to get married and they were alone. I read the vows and each one said "I do." When I pronounced them man and wife, they hugged and kissed.'

Amy then changed into a white vest top and denim shorts and, with her new husband in tow, went to the Big Pink Diner restaurant for a celebration meal. The Big Pink Diner had recently been patronised by Tony Blair while he stayed at Bee Gee Robin Gibb's beach mansion. The married couple arrived back at the hotel separately. Confronted by reporters, Blake said, with a wink, 'We had a good day but I can't really talk about it.' Back together, they repaired to the pool bar and carried on the celebrations. When they tried to head out for another walk, they were caught in a tropical downpour.

With Blake and Amy initially being so coy towards reporters about whether they had indeed wed, the first confirmation came when Blake changed his status on the MySpace website from single to married. Then a spokesperson for the singer confirmed, 'Amy and Blake got married [on Friday]. They are both very happy.' Amy then confirmed the marriage herself, during a concert back in London. 'I don't know if you heard, but I just got married to the best man in the world,' she announced, smiling, to rapturous cheers and applause from the audience, which included Elton John and his partner David Furnish. She also said, with a grin, 'I broke my tooth – it's not pretty. At least I can just about sing.' Also during the concert she ribbed Mitch, who was in the audience, with jokes that he now had to pay for her second wedding.

The couple's parents had neither been informed of nor included in the marriage. Blake's father Giles seemed philosophical about this: 'I spoke to them and they are very happy. We will support him and Amy in whatever they decide to do.' However, Amy's parents were said to be far more hurt at their exclusion. 'I'm not angry, just sad,' said Mitch. 'I would have liked to walk her down the aisle.'

It cannot have been easy for the parents to be excluded and Amy confirms that Mitch was most upset not for himself but for her mother. She hinted that they would try to make it up to them with a second ceremony back in England. 'We're gonna do the whole big thing for everyone over here. But we always knew our ceremony was going to be just about me and Blake. We just wanted to go away and do something with no fuss.' Janis, meanwhile, admits, 'I thought she would lose interest in him. I didn't think they would actually get married.'

On their return to England, the couple went out with Blake's parents to an Indian restaurant, the Mint Leaf, which stands near the A46 road between Lincoln and Newark. Amy's presence raised plenty of eyebrows among the customers and also prompted the *Sunday Mirror* to headline the story with an extraordinary pun: CHICKEN JAZZFREZI, AMY? 'They had booked the Saturday before and the Civils are regular customers, so there was nothing unusual about that,' said the waiter who looked after Amy, who was wearing a green top and tight jeans, and her in-laws. 'It was the first time Amy had met her parents-in-law and we think it's great that they brought her here. I didn't realise who it was at first but customers kept asking and one of our staff members recognised her. After that I was a bit nervous and tried to make everything perfect.

'There was a real buzz in the restaurant that evening and everyone was talking about it,' he added. 'She was fine with all the attention and was getting on very well with the in-laws all night. Everyone left the restaurant with a smile on their face that evening – it was really exciting for all the people there.'

Amy and Blake, too, left the Mint Leaf with smiles on their faces. However, their married bliss was interrupted cruelly on Wednesday, 8 August. It should have been one of the happiest nights of Amy's life. She discovered she had been nominated in three categories at the MTV Video Music Awards. However, she was instead rushed into A&E at University College London Hospital at 1 a.m. A spokesman for Island Records said, 'Amy Winehouse was admitted to UCLH this morning suffering from severe exhaustion.'

However, a fuller story soon emerged. On the Monday she had touched down at Heathrow Airport, after performing at a music festival in Chicago. She and Blake immediately began drinking their way through pubs from Hounslow to Camden. Thus started a three-day binge, during which Amy was said to look 'like a zombie – white as a sheet and trembling'. Towards the end of the session, Amy is said to have taken a drug overdose and later described the experience as 'one of the most terrifying moments of my life'.

She told the *News of the World*, 'I don't know how to explain what happened. I can't remember what I looked like. I couldn't recognise myself. It was terrifying – I was terrified. I was so out of control. It just happened. It shocked me. I'm sorry – I just don't know what got in to me.'

After having her stomach pumped at the UCLH, she was then moved, with one newspaper claiming she was taken to the Priory in Roehampton, and another countering that she was actually recuperating at a luxury Hampshire hotel. Her father Mitchell would not confirm where she was staying, only that he was trying to get his daughter to eat. 'She's skinny as anything and dehydrated and looks like she's just come from a concentration camp,' he said. 'She's barely eating. She's not sleeping. I try to get her to eat but that's easier said than done. I know that if she doesn't eat she's going to die. There's no reason for her to want to self-destruct like this.'

Wherever Amy went immediately after the UCLH, she ultimately ended up at the Causeway Retreat in Essex. It is an apt venue for any celebrity, since it has been written up in some very glamorous publications. *Tatler* magazine says of the Causeway, 'We're confident you'll be in good hands.' *The Sun* describes the centre as 'state-of-the-art' and compares it to a '5-star hotel with a gym, swimming pool and games room', adding that 'it's even got a music therapy room'. London's *Evening Standard* said, 'The Causeway Retreat fans say its location makes it unique. It cuts people off from the world, quite literally, giving a sense of a new beginning.' As for what the Causeway says of itself, its website boasts, 'We have demonstrated great success in helping clients move beyond underlying problems and onto a path of true recovery.'

True recovery was just what the doctor ordered for Amy as she arrived at the Causeway. Within forty-eight hours, she reportedly visited a brain specialist in London for a brain check. This was because, during her overdose, she had experienced a seizure. A neurologist at Queen Hospital explained that this was a routine procedure: 'The brain is an electrical organ so drug use can caused generalised discharges of electricity, presenting as seizures, which can be life-threatening. It's routine for anyone who has suffered a seizure to have a scan for other damage or tumours.'

Asked about this story, Amy's camp gave a firm 'no comment'. However, a source close to Amy did reveal why she left the Causeway. 'She was supposed to stay for a few weeks and sort herself out. But after a couple of decent meals she insisted she was fit to go home. She wanted to leave Tuesday evening. People close to her are devastated. But Blake wants her to return to normality – and we all know what their normality is.'

Not that, it seems, Amy and Blake were particularly missed back at the Causeway. The couple were accused of disturbing the peaceful atmosphere at the retreat, with fingers being particularly pointed at Blake. 'It's supposed to be a peaceful backdrop to help people deal with their problems,' said an insider. 'But Amy and Blake kept rowing and spoiling the ambience. While Amy would be welcomed back with open arms, I'm not sure they'd say the same for Blake.'

It was also said that, although Amy was the one seeking help, it was all too often Blake who hogged the attention. He also apparently upset staff at UCLH, too. This only strengthened the urgent resolve of Amy's family to try to separate the pair, at least while Amy was seeking help. Very soon, that resolve was to become far, far more urgent.

On a Wednesday, in late August, Amy and Blake were staying at London's posh Sanderson Hotel. Called 'A glamorous heaven' by the *Sunday Times Style Magazine*, 'an urban oasis' by *Vanity Fair*, and 'the hippest hotel in the world' by *GQ*, the

Sanderson is one of the capital's swishest hotels. The couple hoped that its opulent splendour would be a suitable venue for them to lick their wounds and recover from the turbulence of recent weeks. They had checked in on the Monday, and, when news reached Amy's brother Alex that they had not left their room for forty-eight hours, he tried to visit his sister to check that all was OK. It is believed that, at Blake's request, Alex was prevented from entering the hotel.

Later that day, Mitch arrived at the hotel and dined with Amy and Blake at one of the Sanderson's posh, exclusive restaurants. He left the hotel around 10 p.m., leaving Amy and Blake seemingly in good spirits as they played pool with friends and continued to drink. Around 11 p.m., Amy met a mystery woman and seemed to take receipt of a package as the pair hugged. In the early hours of the morning, Amy and Blake returned to their hotel room. However, they were not about to retire quietly and the real drama of the evening was just about to start.

An argument broke out between the pair. It was a mighty, vicious, voluminous row that echoed and resounded around the hotel, disturbing other guests. A posh table in the hotel room was smashed during this row and, at about 3 a.m., there was such concern for Amy and so many complaints from other guests about the noise, that the hotel concierge called the police. Soon after this, Amy burst out of the room in floods of tears, with Blake in hot pursuit, screaming after her. They piled into a lift, in which another hotel guest was already travelling. The guest says, 'She was cowering in the corner and I thought he was going to hit her. When the lift door opened, she took off across the lobby at a real pace. He was chasing after her and was about five paces behind by the time she got to the main hotel entrance.'

Amy sprinted down Berners Street and was clearly in a state of total panic. Blake was in hot pursuit still but could not catch up. An eyewitness says, 'Amy was so hell-bent on getting away from him that she ran into the middle of the street and flagged down a random car that happened to be full of girls. She was saying, "Quickly, I have to get in, I have to get away, please help me." Her voice was breaking. You could tell she was scared.'

Amy was allowed into the car, which set off at great speed, leaving Blake trailing in its wake. Amy was dropped off outside Charing Cross train station and she walked into a twenty-four-hour shop and bought some cigarettes. 'She was looking completely out of her head,' said a fellow shopper.

Meanwhile, Blake had been left behind and was staggering around in a total daze, trying to find Amy. He wandered around looking in doorways and down alleys. From time to time he shouted her name, but to no avail, of course. He also repeatedly tried to call her on her mobile phone. Eventually, he managed to get through to her by phone. A tense and loud conversation ensued. After the pair calmed down, they arranged to meet up at around 4 a.m. They then walked back to the hotel, arm in arm, at around 4.45 a.m.

However, any hope that they could put this latest drama behind them was vain indeed. The entire fight had been played out in front of not just the public, but also in front of press photographers who had snapped plenty of photographs of Amy and Blake. The two were covered in blood and scratches. Amy also had blood pouring through her silk ballet shoes, leading to speculation that she had been injecting heroin in between her toes. They talk about washing your dirty linen in public – this was more like washing your *bloodstained* linen in public.

Naturally, the press went immediately to town on the story. On hearing of the drama, Mitch rushed immediately to the hotel to be at his daughter's side. So concerned was he for her wellbeing that he even investigated legal routes to get her and Blake apart.

'Mitch is desperate for Amy to get some proper lengthy treatment but she'll only do it with Blake. Mitch even looked to see if he could get a restraining order against him but it's legally impossible,' said a source. The police did, though, arrive and later announced, 'After receiving a complaint from a third party, police spoke with a woman but she made no allegation of criminal offences.' The room that Amy and Blake had been staying in was reportedly a mess. A source at the hotel said that the bedroom and bathroom had bloodstains in them. One – highly doubtful – report claimed that the damage came to £9,000. 'The in-house cleaners were totally shocked when they entered the room. I've certainly never seen anything like it before,' said the source. 'They had to get an outside firm to clean blood off the walls and then there was a hefty paint job.'

After speaking to Mitch, Amy and Blake left the hotel on Thursday morning in a silver Mercedes. Naturally, the press obsession with the story was to go on for days. Many reports suggested that Blake might have beaten up Amy. But she was quick to dispute these claims, using a seemingly unconventional route to do so.

Mario Lavandeira, better known as Perez Hilton, is a celebrity blogger. Based in Los Angeles, California, he has built up an extraordinary level of contacts and influence in the world of showbiz. His blog was originally called PageSixSixSix.com – after the Page Six gossip column of the *New York Post* – and is now known simply as perezhilton.com. He claims to have up to 8 million page views in any twenty-four-hour period. He has become close friends with the US socialite Paris Hilton – hence his nickname – and is often turned to by celebrities across the globe who wish to get their story out to the masses quickly, and with some control over the message.

It was Perez Hilton that Amy turned to when she wished to dispute reports that Blake had beaten her up during their infamous stay at the Sanderson Hotel. She sent a series of text messages to Hilton, asking him to put the truth up on his website. 'Blake is the best man in the world,' read one such text. 'We would never ever harm each other... I was cutting myself after he found me in our room about to do drugs with a call girl and rightly said I wasn't good enough for him. I lost it and he saved my life.'

Amy then said that, far from hurting her, Blake had actually been responsible for saving her life. She wrote,

He did not and never has hurt me. He has such a hard time and he is so supportive... He is an amazing man who saved my life again and got cut badly for his troubles. All he gets is horrible stories printed about him and he just keeps quiet, but this is too much. I'll be alright. I need to fight my man's corner for him though.

It is hardly surprising that there was so much concern for Amy's wellbeing, particularly given that the episode happened while they stayed in a hotel. Time after time, Amy and Blake's relationship has been compared to that of Sex Pistols member Sid Vicious and his girlfriend Nancy Spungen. 'Sid and Nancy' – as they are always referred to – also had a high-profile and notorious relationship. They seemed stuck in a cycle of self-destruction, drug abuse and violence. In October 1978, the couple checked into room 100 of the Hotel Chelsea in New York City. One morning, Vicious awoke from a drug-induced stupor to discover his girlfriend dead on the bathroom floor. She had a single stab wound to her lower abdomen. The bed was also stained with blood. Vicious was later charged with murder, received bail and then died from a heroin overdose.

Following all the drama that Amy and Blake had been through, there was major disappointment but very little surprise when Amy decided to postpone her impending tour of the USA and Canada. It was not an easy decision to make but Amy, ever the perfectionist, decided that she would rather wait until she was ready to do herself and her fans justice, rather than turn up and give a half-hearted performance. Her camp said, 'Due to the rigours involved in touring, Amy Winehouse has been advised to postpone her upcoming September US and Canadian tour dates... Plans are being made to reschedule her US tour for early 2008. Until then, Amy has been ordered to rest and is working with medical professionals to address her health.'

The venue for that rest could hardly have been more tranquil and beautiful. High on Morne Chastanet, overlooking St Lucia and the Caribbean, the Jade Mountain resort is utterly luxurious and mesmerising. The spacious, grand rooms each have their own private swimming pool and breathtaking views. Amy hoped their break at the £700-a-night resort would prove to be a therapeutic one. At last, she hoped, they could put their problems behind them and move onwards and upwards to a greater future. However, according to some accounts, their stay proved far from healthy.

Reports soon surfaced that Amy had not merely vomited over her room, but had vomited blood. A hotel worker said, 'There was blood and vomit all over the bathroom; it was just terrible. It looked like she'd been sick many times. There was blood mixed up in the vomit. It was sickening. They were horrified by the state of the room, which looked like a bomb had hit it.' The hotel's manager offered to send for a doctor but Amy declined. 'She said she'd be fine,' said the worker. 'Everyone was concerned because she looked so frail.'

Amy was also sick over a sofa while drinking in the restaurant at the resort. This time, the smell of her vomit was said to be so overpowering that the restaurant had to be completely closed while it was cleaned. Once it reopened, Amy caused a few concerns by reappearing with Blake. She ate a Caesar salad and Blake wolfed down a steak. They returned soon after and Amy tucked into a burger and a salad. Luckily, she managed to hold her food down. Summing up their stay, the hotel source told the *Daily Mirror*, 'They're not like our typical guests. They stand out because they're both covered in cuts and have tattoos all over their bodies. They both behave very strangely.'

Admittedly, the newspaper headlines that screamed, AMY AND BLAKE'S BLOODBATH CONTINUES and AMY SECONDS FROM DEATH were somewhat over the top, but Amy was by this time handing new scandals to the press on a plate. It seems certain that some of the coverage was exaggerated or fabricated, but a lot of it was accurate. For the press – who had grown tired of Pete Doherty since he split with Kate Moss, and with David Beckham, who was LA-bound – Amy was proving to be the new tabloid obsession. Once the tabloids have their claws into someone, it rarely ends in anything but tears for their victim. The press have without doubt made up a lot of the coverage they have awarded Amy and Blake's relationship, especially about their hedonism and alleged weight issues.

All too often, Blake has been cast as the bad guy. 'He's not very good for her on a professional level,' Sky News entertainment man Neil Sean said, 'but she's so hooked in deep she can't stop the – I suppose – the love that she's got for him.'

However, jumping to this conclusion seems unfair on both

Blake and Amy. Whatever his failings, Blake has stuck by Amy's side and is clearly besotted with his lady. Moreover, to cast Amy as his unwitting victim insults her, casting her as a helpless little lady. All the evidence of Amy's life suggests she is far away from this. 'I think those close to us know the truth,' says Blake. 'It's not one long drink-and-drug party for us, and, as for the weight issues, it's just not like that – we're actually quite a nice and normal couple at home.'

Amy echoed Blake's attempt to portray them as a normal couple. 'I'm sorted out. Nothing's wrong with me... A lot of fuss has been made about nothing,' she shrugged.

Mitchell hoped that these 'all is fine' statements were accurate, though his hope was not without qualification: 'I don't know what they've been doing for the last month or so. We'd like to think that she and Blake have stayed clean since they went to St Lucia. But the thing with drug addicts is that they rarely tell you the truth.'

Happily, before long the tabloids were forced to write a positive story about Amy when she collected yet more laurels. At the MOBO awards, she was handed the Best Female Singer gong. At the O^2 arena (formerly the Millennium Dome), she sang 'Me and Mr Jones' and 'Tears Dry on Their Own'. When she took to the stage to collect her award, she kept her speech short and sweet, merely saying thank you and then returning to her table. She couldn't be blamed for being so short: after all that had been written about her in recent months, Amy was just keen to avoid further controversy.

On the same night, she won the Vodafone Live Award,

beating off the likes of Lily Allen, K T Tunstall and Kate Nash. Amy sent the landlord of the Hawley Arms to collect her prize in her stead. 'We'll be putting it behind the bar,' he quipped at the ceremony at Brompton Hall in West London.

These successes made up for the disappointment at losing out to the Klaxons in the Mercury Prize earlier that month. She won a standing ovation for her performance at the ceremony at the Grosvenor House Hotel. She sang 'Love is a Losing Game', stripping the song back to its acoustic roots and sending a wave of emotion across the venue. Jools Holland, the compere, said after the performance: 'Amy Winehouse... one of the most amazing voices. I've worked with a lot of people and I'm telling you, she's got one of the most amazing voices of all time.'

However, when it came to the award, it went to the three-piece Klaxons. The band's lead singer Jamie Reynolds said he was 'not surprised' that Amy did not win. He said, 'When I came off stage I was upset because I thought she gave a fantastic performance and I absolutely loved her record, but her recording is retro and ours is a forward-thinking record and that's what the Mercury Prize stands for.'

Polydor co-president Colin Barlow said, 'A lot of people thought it was going to be the Amy Winehouse Mercurys, but the great thing about the awards is that they are about innovation.' Music industry commentators added that perhaps Amy had missed out because her suitability for the prize made her a too obvious choice – especially given the predictable victory of Arctic Monkeys the previous year.

However, Dan Cairns of the *Sunday Times* 'Culture' section, did speak up for Amy:

> You can tell Klaxons' hearts are in the right place and they obviously love being in a band and making the music they make, but to propose that *Myths*... is the best album in the past 12 months is just nuts. It's got about two songs on and then acres of sonic mush, albeit fun mush. Bat For Lashes or Amy should have won.

Blake was more concise and direct in his support. 'Amy was robbed,' he spat. 'Who knows why they didn't give her the award. But I was so proud of her for her performance. She's really well and she doesn't need to go back into rehab.'

Meanwhile, Girls Aloud's Cheryl Cole also spoke up for Amy. 'I was glad to see Amy Winehouse looking better at the Mercury awards,' she said. 'I didn't hear her singing but she looked amazing in the pictures. She's got deep issues to deal with but seems to have a strong support network in her family. Her dad seems a decent guy.'

Janice Turner was less kind in *The Times*, writing that Amy 'resembled a Barbie doll attacked by an additive-high, felt-tip-wielding toddler'. Her feelings were echoed more sensitively by the US singer Rihanna, who said, 'I'm worried about Amy. I want her to get better, as I love her. There's no a doubt in my mind she can still be successful in America even though she's been linked to drugs. It'd be awesome to go on tour with her in the States. I'd love her to join me.'

In the wake of her appearance, a BBC journalist commented, 'She's become such a worshipped and tortured enigma that her appearances now seem like visitations from some sort of mythical figure.' Even Rabbi Aryeh Sufrin, founder of Drugsline, stuck his oar in and offered his help to Amy. The rabbi warned readers, 'This just shows that the Jewish community is not immune to addiction.' *Jewish News* editor Zeddy Lawrence said that Sufrin told him that he was more than happy to help Amy and Blake. 'If they reach out then my door is open to them,' he told Lawrence.

As for record executives at Amy's label, they were insistent that they were doing all they could to support her. There had been chatter in some quarters insinuating that perhaps they were secretly turning a blind eye to her addiction, or even quietly encouraging it because they felt it made her a more newsworthy proposition. Promoter Raye Cosbert brushes all this away. 'We've been doing everything we can to help with Amy's personal problems over the past few weeks,' he insisted. 'We've advised her to take complete rest during this difficult period and have put all her promotional commitments on hold. How can it be in Island's interests to have Amy dead when the company's hoping for five more platinum albums?'

As for Amy's and Blake's parents, they were understandably terrified by what they were hearing about their loved ones' antics. Blake's stepfather Giles Civil said, 'You couldn't tell Sid Vicious what to do, could you? But I'd like Blake and Amy to think about those two. It might shake them up. I doubt it, but maybe. I think they both need to get medical help, before one of them, if not both of them, eventually die. We're concerned that if one of them dies, the other will die. They are a very close couple, and if one dies through substance abuse, the other may commit suicide.

'They're living in a world where access to drugs is easy. They have plenty of money available and what they need, what they want, they can have without question. They're going through abject denial at the moment. They don't see themselves as having a problem and are quite aggressive in defence of themselves. They believe they're recreational users of drugs but it seems to us this is not the case and clearly they are addicts.'

He then proposed a novel step to help shake some sense back into them. 'We urge Amy's fans to send a message to her that her addiction is not acceptable. I would not want any harm to come to Amy and Blake but perhaps it's time to stop buying her records. We should not be condoning her addiction by awarding her either record sales or industry awards.'

Mitch added that he had spoken to Amy and she 'sounded fine. We're not talking about people who are in imminent danger of death. Physically, she's not fantastic, but while she was away I think the eating disorder was worked on, and she put on a stone. In the space of eight days, that's pretty good. It's no good blaming anyone and saying in the last four months, Blake's got worse because of Amy and she's got worse because of Blake. In the last four months, they have got worse. They are a married couple, they love each other, although there are issues if they feel they've got to cut themselves to show it. If it means they get cured together, I hope they get cured together.

'If it means that they get cured by being separated, then so be it. But nobody can physically separate them. Blake's parents can't take him back to Nottingham if he doesn't want to go and I can't force Amy to do anything. I've tried. It doesn't work. The doctors said, "You've tried the screaming and shouting, it doesn't work. We've got to try gentle persuasion, let them feel they're making the decisions." Guess what: that hasn't worked either.'

As for Amy, she was insistent that she had no intention whatsoever of breaking up with Blake. Indeed, she argued that, far from being the source of her problems, he was the greatest hope she had of overcoming them. 'I can't beat drugs without him. He's my rock and as a married couple we need to go through everything together. Blake says he isn't going back to rehab – but I can if I want. But I'm not going without him. I know I need help, but Blake's the only one who can help me. I don't want to lose him. I won't lose him. I want to make him happy – like what he does to me. I feel disgusting and Blake's the only one who stops me feeling like this. I can't believe he even wants to be with me. I don't understand why. All I know is I'm the luckiest girl alive to have someone as caring as Blake,' she added.

However, some of this was falling on deaf ears, as was shown in December 2007 when her mother Janis wrote Amy an open letter via the pages of the *News of the World*. This is what she said:

Blake, your husband, might not be my favourite person – you know that, Amy – but he's your choice and I would never say anything about him to hurt you. When I was quoted recently as saying 'Thank God Blake's inside' what I meant was that putting him in jail might help him to clean up HIS act and change HIS life.

It wasn't said out of viciousness or to upset you. If your relationship is meant to be, it will survive. I'm a great believer that everything in life happens for a reason, a purpose. And if you two are destined to be together forever, then so be it. But I want you to love Blake for who he is, Amy. Not because you feel sorry for him, or because he can get you doped up. Not for any other reason than that you have respect for him.

Janis was referring to an interview Mitchell had given to Fern Britton. Britton asked, 'So she is still drinking?'

Mitch replied, 'She's not drinking as heavily now as she was then actually but there are other problems. The other problem is the bulimia, which is still apparent, although she's put on about a stone in weight but it's still affecting her health; and there are problems with substance abuse as well. But, again, not as bad as has been reported.

'It's apparent in her music that she's smoked dope for quite a while, probably from the age of sixteen or seventeen, perhaps even earlier. She was a complete opponent of hard drugs – in fact, she got up and said she couldn't understand why people in the music industry took hard drugs – and that changed about six months ago when she got married to Blake. And I'm not saying its Blake's fault. What I'm saying is Amy's responsible for her own actions. However, it's a fact that the hard drugs coincided with their marriage. Well, I knew that they were going to get married, we weren't completely in the dark but we were kind of hoping that Amy's mum could have been there at least. So we were a little disappointed, yeah.'

He continued, 'I don't read the papers myself. A friend of mine, a guy called Ginger Norman, he reads them for me. Because I can't bring myself to read the papers every day and he kind of vets the news for me every day because I just can't face it. He asked me to have a look at this particular piece, which I did do. I phoned the newspaper in question, spoke to the newsdesk. I told them what had happened. They said they had no interest in what I have to say on this subject.'

Soon after the interview, speaking about Blake, Mitchell also told the *Star*,

'He doesn't get Brownie points off me for that, he's normally smashed off his face too, and the only reason he wasn't passed out on the floor was because either his drugs hadn't kicked in yet or he'd run out of them. The way I see it is if he hadn't been there, she probably wouldn't have put all that junk inside her in the first place.

'If Blake were to go to jail for GBH it would probably be the best thing that could happen for Amy... She'd be mortified if he did go to jail but it would be a chance for her to get on the straight and narrow.

'The trouble is Blake seems to want them to go to rehab together and to be in control – and they've been told that isn't a good idea and the likelihood of recovery is small. If he were in jail for a few months I think Amy would have a better chance of recovering. She needs to get herself sorted before she worries about him.'

Better news came in the shape of Amy's settlement with songwriter and producer P*Nut over a claim for copyright infringement. P*Nut, whose real name is John Harrison, said he and Amy co-wrote the song 'He Can Only Hold Her' in his studio in 2006. P*Nut's solicitor, Bob Page, of Jayes and Page, said, 'This represents a very satisfactory outcome for P*Nut, who considered his contribution to the song to be perfectly obvious. He was therefore extremely disappointed not to receive the credit he deserved on Amy's album and furthermore at the extent of the resistance he encountered in securing his fair share of the copyright. Whilst Amy and her publishers took the matter to the brink, P*Nut is pleased that common sense has prevailed and he is now looking forward to seeing his contribution properly recognised on future exploitation of this song.'

There was also a light-hearted moment when Amy complained that her songs were being used in scenes during the TV soap *Emmerdale*, in the Woolpack pub. 'Amy's very image-conscious. When she licensed her songs for commercial use, she probably wanted a lucrative advertising campaign – not a soap full of Yorkshire farmers,' said a source.

In October, Amy was up for yet another gong. This time she was nominated for the Best Album category in the Q Awards. Previous Q winners include U2, the Rolling Stones, Oasis,

Coldplay, Radiohead, The Who and Arctic Monkeys. Down the years, there have been plenty of exciting moments at Q Awards ceremonies: Pogues hellraiser Shane MacGowan set Bono's hair alight; Oasis singer Liam Gallagher attacked photographers with a steel pole and had pops at both Coldplay's Chris Martin and Robbie Williams; Elton John had a pop at Madonna.

She was up against some formidable opposition: the previous year's winners in this category, Arctic Monkeys' 'Favourite Worst Nightmare'; Kaiser Chiefs' 'Yours Truly, Angry Mob'; Arcade Fire's 'Neon Bible'; Manic Street Preachers' 'Send Away the Tigers'.

Amy didn't attend the lunchtime ceremony at the Grosvenor House Hotel due to illness. Naturally, this raised eyebrows and headlines far out of proportion. The *Now* magazine website screamed, AMY WINEHOUSE STICKS TWO FINGERS UP AT Q AWARDS. Mark Ronson collected the award on her behalf and said, 'That's Amy – taking her pain and turmoil and making it into music we enjoy.'

Television star Jonathan Ross took the opportunity to crack a few jokes in the absence of Amy. He said, 'I was on a three-to-one bet that Amy would die before Pavarotti. I'm really annoyed with Amy that I lost.' Later on in the evening, he also joked about Led Zeppelin's forthcoming December 2007 reunion at the O$_2$, saying, 'There were millions of hits on the website to register for tickets to their gig. It was probably all the Parkinson's sufferers clicking the mouse more than they should.' Nice!

Other winners on the night included Kate Nash, who won Breakthrough Artist; the Q Lifetime Achievement went to Johnny Marr of the Smiths; and the Q Idol was Kylie Minogue. There had been precious little controversy on the night. The best the following morning's papers could muster was that the name of Arctic Monkeys was misspelled on their gong.

The award that Amy won became the subject of something of a mystery following the ceremony, when it went missing. Mark Ronson seemed to lose it and then there were varying reports of who had last seen it with comedians Alan Carr and Ricky Gervais rumoured to have been the last people who had laid eyes on it.

The award finally emerged and in the strangest of places. Andrew Morris, owner of Bar Soho in Old Compton Street in London's West End, found it in the toilets of his bar in the early hours of the morning following the ceremony. 'I thought it wasn't real when I first saw it,' he revealed. 'But then I looked at the newspapers and saw the Q Awards were on last night and Amy Winehouse didn't collect her prize.' Then he recalled seeing Ronson partying at his bar and it all fell into place. 'I'm sure the state Amy's in these days I'm sure she doesn't care too much,' he said of his find. 'But I'm sure the Q Awards organisers wouldn't be too happy if it's been left in a bar. If Amy's getting an award she should really be there to pick it up.' The story was run in the *Metro* newspaper under the headline THE Q FOR THE LOO.

Around this time, two men from the music industry took the opportunity to have a pop at Amy about her personal life.

Both instances reeked of hypocrisy. Francis Rossi was one of the co-founders of the rock band Status Quo. He sang lead vocals and played lead guitar with the band. Now approaching his sixties, he likes to think of himself as an elder statesman of rock. Rossi said, 'Amy is supposed to be great but I can't stick her. I like a couple of records but I'm not sure if people will like her in three years. I'm not knocking her for the sake of it. But I have been subjected to so much of Amy and her antics that I just think, "Fuck off".

'What message does giving her Woman of the Year send to young people? There has to be some responsibility somewhere, surely. Everyone knew what was going on with her. She's not a good role model. They should have said to her, "You're not getting it. You would have done but you're not cutting it any more."

'She may be able to sing, but what gets through to the kids in the street is the fact that she's out of her tree, falling over and not being able to keep her hands out of her knickers. She should straighten herself out.' He then turned to Pete Doherty, saying, 'He, on the other hand, isn't even worth entertaining. At least Amy has serious talent. Pete hasn't got anything. There's no talent there, otherwise he would do something. He doesn't count. He seems quite intelligent but the records are grim.'

Next to have a dig at Amy was Ian Brown. Having first come to public attention as the frontman of the Mancunian band the Stone Roses, Brown is nowadays a solo artist. Of Amy, he said, 'I think she's an absolute sucker. The girl's got all those tattoos in the last few years – and one day she's gonna go, "Oh, no!" Suckers. Anyone who drinks to that condition is a sucker. They're scared of living.'

Perhaps what really sucked, though, was the hypocrisy of Rossi and Brown. Rossi has long boasted of his own drug-fuelled exploits during the band's heyday. Asked if he enjoyed cocaine use, he boasted, 'Fucking right. By the mid seventies I had an astonishing cocaine habit. I'd go out for the night, come back, go to bed at some godforsaken hour and my head would be going like a steam hammer.' He has also admitted that he lost part of the septum of his nose, watching it wash down a plughole as he showered. Brown, too, has made no secret of his extensive drug use, though his drug of choice is cannabis.

Therefore, for either of these men to criticise Amy for her partying was as clear a case as one can imagine of the pot calling the kettle black. Perhaps there was also an element of envy in their words: seeing an artist and human being in her prime firing up the green-eyed monster in artists who had long since seen their best days. More reasoned, measured and admirable words came from the mouth of another veteran rocker, Mick Jagger of the Rolling Stones. Jagger dabbled with drugs during the heyday of his own band but there was no hypocrisy in his statement about Amy.

Jagger said, 'Amy is a brilliant artist who makes fantastic music. She has class. But I'm worried she might die if she goes down the road that she's taken. If only she would sort herself out. It's hard, as your mind has to make that switch. If my mind hadn't always told me that I should not do too much, I could have ended up like Amy years ago. But I always had that voice in my head that kept me on my toes and told me to stop altogether in the end. I realised I didn't want to die young.'

Duran Duran's singer Simon Le Bon had similar thoughts. 'I'd like to sit her down, put some warm clothes on her, get her out of her bloodstained crap, give her a bath, put some food in her. Even if she doesn't die of a drug overdose, she's going to die of malnutrition. That's what worries me. What happened to those fabulous tits?'

On the evening following the Q Awards, which Amy had missed due to illness, she seemed to have recovered when she appeared at Harvey Nichols for the launch of a new collection by Mary-Kate and Ashley Olsen called the Row. 'The twins were really looking forward to meeting Amy,' said a source. 'They spent all night chatting.' Amy then embarked on a three-hour shopping spree in the posh clothes store. She bagged clothes and toiletries for her and Blake.

'The shop stayed open until 1.30 a.m. for her,' said an employee. 'She was having a great time. Blake was running around after her.'

However, according to a different eyewitness, Blake had got bored of the shopping and ducked off in a taxi with Lily Cole and another mystery girl. Another onlooker sourly commented that, during the dinner with the Olsen twins, Amy's fingers had looked dirty and stained.

Amid growing fears that she was going off the rails, she did exactly that – but not in the way people expected. She was on her way to Paris to attend some fashion shows and, after going through the security barrier at the Waterloo Eurostar, she seemingly had a change of heart and decided not to travel. She illegally leapt over the station's security barrier and ran back into the main concourse of Waterloo station. Amy had arrived at the station looking tearful and it is thought that her change of mind came about because she did not wish to be parted from Blake.

A passenger said, 'Amy was crying, gesticulating wildly and shouting while the man with her was trying to calm her and get her through the gate. She mentioned Blake's name more than once.

'Eventually they went through security, but then Amy came running back. She hurdled the security gate then ran up the escalator, shouting and screaming, into Waterloo station concourse. It was quite a sight – this tiny girl with a massive beehive leaping over a barrier. It was pretty clear she was not keen on getting on that train to Paris.'

As Amy ran off, a policeman chased after her. A London Transport Police spokesperson confirmed, 'We spoke to a twenty-four-year-old female at the Eurostar entrance yesterday. She wasn't detained and no further action was taken.' In the end Amy was persuaded to travel after all and she got on the train to Paris.

On her return to England, Amy hit the headlines again when she and Blake hung out with fresh-from-rehab Pete Doherty at his pad in Wiltshire. As he recorded an interview with the radio station Xfm, Doherty said, 'Apparently I have self-esteem issues.' Once more, rumours went around that

Amy and Doherty planned to work together, prompting further concern in the press at the thought of two such hedonistic artists joining forces. 'She plays better than James Brown playing acoustic guitar. She thinks she's shit, but she's not,' said Babyshambles guitarist Mick Whitnall of Amy's guitar skills. 'I've never met a girl who plays like that, let alone a man,' he added.

Doherty said that a track entitled '1939 Returning' was one of the new songs he had been working on. 'I'm going to try to get Miss Winehouse to help me with it, hopefully,' he said. Soon there were rumours that she and Pete would duet at an MTV awards ceremony. A source said, 'MTV have been trying to persuade Amy to go for ages. When she heard Pete was doing it she thought it could be a laugh. Amy and Pete are going to get together and see if they can work out a duet and get it on the schedule. The organisers wanted to add a bit of danger to what is the squeaky-clean boy band of award shows. They've certainly done that. I just hope they know what they've let themselves in for. They've been jamming for ages with the plan to perform together. This would be a pretty high-profile place to do it.'

Pete Doherty was asked what advice he would offer Amy during her hour of need. 'I wouldn't give her any,' he snapped. 'She's fine. It's all bollocks. People should leave her alone. I went for a drink with her earlier today and she's totally fine. Perfectly healthy and happy. People are saying she's out of control, but she's not. She's a sensible girl and she knows what she's doing. She ain't doing nothing wrong.'

However, Doherty's words of reassurance could do nothing to stop the avalanche of concern that was coming down on Amy's head – particularly when reports threw up fresh concern that she was self-harming again. A tabloid photographer snapped her while out shopping in Covent Garden and noticed some red lines on her hands. It was hard to tell whether they were just lines of lipstick or scars. Another snapper around the same time pictured her retrieving a cigarette she had accidentally dropped into the gutter. NO BUTTS, AMY... THAT'S FILTHY! screamed the *Daily Mirror*, unaware that many consider the tabloid press itself to be firmly positioned in the gutter.

Asked about these latest reports, Mitchell revealed, 'I wrote a eulogy for Amy myself last month. When she had her seizure and was taken to hospital, I really thought that could be it. The doctors told us even a whiff of another drug could kill her.'

By this time, tabloid fascination in Amy was huge. Even her buying some McDonald's food while out on tour in Germany was deemed worthy of a story in the newspapers. Earlier in the month, a visit to McDonald's by Amy and Blake in London had also hit the newspapers. On that occasion she had been travelling to a photoshoot in Hoxton and was laden with boxes of Betsey Johnson shoes. Then she was spotted eating in a Soho restaurant. 'Amy came in really good spirits and ordered an extra-large portion of brown stew chicken, which she polished off in minutes,' said a fellow diner. 'She was looking really healthy and it's clear she's putting on weight again.'

She was also spotted pounding away on a running machine

shortly before her Berlin concert. Her health kick also involved one-on-one tuition with yoga guru David Sye, who is based in her hometown of Camden and has previously trained the likes of the fashion designer and actress Sadie Frost.

'Amy has been having regular one-on-one sessions with David for five weeks now,' said a source. 'It's been a big step for Amy and one that could play a huge role in her eventually beating her demons. She pops into his studio for sessions but has also been calling him regularly on the phone for spiritual advice. Her health has improved over the last few weeks and she has been looking a lot more glowing and healthy. She has started to worry about her health, so she's lucky to have found something that works for her right on her doorstep.'

Her European tour hit a snag when Amy arrived in Norway. She and Blake were relaxing with a friend in the SAS Hotel, in Bergen, in southwestern Norway, when police knocked on the door. The police claim they found seven grams of cannabis in the room and arrested the trio. According to one person present, 'When the police entered the hotel corridor, they quickly noticed a heavy marijuana odour. They knocked on the hotel room door and were met by a very wobbly pop star.'

Another eyewitness described the scene as 'like something from the action movie *Lethal Weapon*, as most of the city's police force turned out – with an ambulance'. The source added that Amy 'had problems remaining on her feet when she opened the door and saw the uniformed police. Making matters even worse, [she] was so intoxicated she experienced great difficulties communicating with the police officers.' Indeed, it is believed that police were forced to wait until 11 p.m. before interviewing her, such was her state.

They were kept in police custody overnight and then fined and released. Amy and Blake were ordered to pay £350 between them, while the other arrested man was fined £240. Prosecutor Lars Morten Lothe explained how the police came to be knocking on Amy's door and what happened next: 'We had a tip from a good source, which led to police checking up on the tip. She spent a few hours in custody from Thursday evening to early Friday; she got a fine and then she was released. They signed a ticket, a fine, at the police station some hours ago. It is a closed case.'

When Amy left police custody she was reportedly in a confused state and asked for a cab to take her back to her hotel. Instead, she was given directions for the short walk back to the hotel.

Mitchell had flown to Bergen to offer his support but the trio had already been freed by the time he arrived. Despite the prosecutor's valiant attempts to prevent the matter being blown out of all proportion, the press naturally went to town on the story. AMY WINEHOUSE GOES TO POT, yelled *E! Online*. WINEHOUSE ARRESTED OVER DRUGS, screamed the *Daily Star* in a story that included yet more predictions that she is 'heading for an early grave'. Even the hotel trade media got in on the act, with a journalist for the online *Hotel Chatter* saying, 'What is shocking is that it was just weed. Doesn't Amy do like harder Class-A type of drugs? And we also learned that Amy doesn't mind shacking up in Radissons but perhaps in the future Amy should check into more drug-friendly hotels.'

Immediately there were fears that the arrest might lead Amy to cancel the following evening's appearance at the Bergen Live rock festival. However, as we've seen often, she genuinely adores performing live and sees it as the best part of her job. Frank Nes, head promoter of Bergen Live, said she had been quick to reassure him that her performance would go ahead. 'We spoke to her management this morning and there isn't anything that would indicate she won't sing tonight. It's not that dramatic, but it's not a pleasant situation for anyone involved.'

It also emerged that Amy was used by police as an example to a rookie officer of how people look when they are under the influence of drugs. 'They are very strict about drug taking in Norway,' said a police source.

With her past record they thought there was more than just a couple of spliffs. When she opened the hotel room door it was obvious she was wasted. She was mumbling and no one could understand her. Amy and Blake were put in separate cells but Amy couldn't be interviewed straightaway because she was totally incoherent. She was cooperative and even let an officer in training look in her eyes so he could recognise how a person high on drugs looks.'

She returned to the hotel and quickly recovered from the ordeal – she ordered champagne in the hotel spa. Mitchell reflected, 'Well, you know, I try to speak to her every other day but, you know, every day I'm in contact with the tour. I went to Norway last week because there was a problem out there. Again, it was in all the newspapers that they found cannabis. It didn't belong to her: it belonged to someone else on the tour. They arrested Blake, Amy and the person who was responsible. And they only released them after they signed a form, which they were told was a release form – it was in Norwegian. It was actually a confession, so this is being dealt with now by the Norwegian authorities and the British Consulate because the ramifications of that is that she now can't get into the States and she was meant to go next week.'

Amy was far from being the first pop star to get on the wrong side of Scandinavian law in recent times. Rapper Snoop Dogg was arrested in March for suspected drug use, and Pete Doherty was arrested and fined in Sweden the previous year. In Doherty's case, he was fined £1,000 after police found traces of cocaine in his blood, following a performance by his rock band at the Hultsfred music festival. Police detained the twenty-seven-year-old Babyshambles frontman after the concert because 'he showed signs of being under the influence of narcotics', Ulf Karlsson, a police spokesman in the city of Kalmar on Sweden's southeastern coast, said.

Amy shrugs off her brushes with the law. 'Life's short,' she says, 'and I've made a lot of mistakes. I was quite self-destructive. I was just doing one destructive thing after the other. I always say I don't regret things and I don't say sorry, but I do really. I believe everything happens for a reason.'

A source close to her said, 'This tour started pretty much as the last one ended. Berlin was a difficult time for everyone and we thought it was going to turn into another tour full of drunken and missed shows. But she's now said that she will not drink before her gigs for the rest of the tour. She stuck to it in Amsterdam, amazingly, and gave her best show of the tour yet. Everyone just hopes she keeps it up.'

Amy told the organiser of her Amsterdam concert about her new pre-gig booze ban. Jan Willem Luyken said, 'She wasn't drunk when she came in and she did not drink backstage. I don't think she was stoned, either. People were joking about her sober performance. They said, "Has the wine bar been closed today?" But, no, she was sober till after her performance. She said she won't drink before shows any more – only afterwards.'

So much for the European leg of her tour. Any hopes Amy had of remaining sober once she returned home took a hit when she learned that Girls Aloud's Sarah Harding had bought a new pad in Camden Town. Harding has long been a mainstay in the tabloid press's 'caner leagues'. She says, 'I have a bit of a binge but I think everyone does, get smashed, they get pie-eyed. I don't go out as often as most girls my age, but when I do I get persecuted for it.'

Not that she was about to deny that she liked a good bender. 'I can drink with the best of them and I like to be able to hold my own. But I regret it the next day when my head's down the bog.' Revealing that her home was near the Hawley Arms pub, Harding quipped, 'I'm in walking distance of the Hawley, which is a bit scary!'

Called 'the home of the "Camden caners"', the Hawley Arms has long been a regular haunt for Amy. For years the Hawley had been something of a nonentity, certainly when compared with other Camden bars such as the Dublin Castle and the Good Mixer. The former was where Madness launched their career and the latter was the scene of numerous battles among the Britpop crowd during the 1990s.

The Hawley now has the chance to become just as legendary thanks to Amy's patronage of it. As the *Independent* reported,

Winehouse, 23, is such a regular she could be made its honorary life president. Her deputy could be Kelly Osbourne, a favoured drinking partner, or Peaches Geldof, another customer. The celebrity endorsements keep coming, though the punters hate comparisons made with the Met Bar, the hotel lounge where celebrities used to fall over themselves to get seen. They think there is a bit more grit to the Hawley.

You don't have to be in skinny-tight jeans and a washed-out T-shirt to drink here, but it helps. Indie haircuts are welcome, too – though customers will tell you that Winehouse's matty beehive and extravagant tattoos are to marvel at, not imitate.

Among regulars who have drunk alongside Amy are Oasis frontman Liam Gallagher and his wife Nicole Appleton, television comedian Noel Fielding, Razorlight's Johnny Borrell and his movie star girlfriend Kirsten Dunst.

The *Evening Standard* rated it London's best pub for star spotting:

This 'proper boozer' last week saw Kate Moss, Primal Scream frontman Bobby Gillespie, Sadie Frost, Amy Winehouse and Kelly Osbourne spend an evening there – together. Osbourne, for one, is a regular player on the pub's 'awesome' jukebox and the likes of Razorlight's Johnny Borrell and (of course) Pete Doherty have also been spotted.

Amy was at one point banned from the pub. 'The manager and his staff are at their wits' end with Amy and her pals. They hate them coming in and have just been waiting for an excuse to throw them out. Amy's hangers-on were throwing stuff out of the window and being a nuisance. Eventually the manager ordered them all out and Amy was told to sort it out or she wouldn't ever be allowed back.'

However, within no time at all, Amy seemed to have charmed the bar management enough not just to let her drink there but to serve behind the bar too! 'Amy treated the pub like her own home, pouring herself vodka Red Bull drinks and choosing the music on the pub iPod,' an onlooker reported. 'She poured shots and, pointing to a black sambuca, told punters, "This is on the house!"'

But while she was seemingly in her element as centre-stage in a thronging London pub, Amy had long been dreaming of success on another continent – that fabled market that is considered such a difficult one to succeed in but one that promises riches of every kind to anyone who does make it there.

Amy Winehouse had her sights set on America.

Chapter Eight

THE AMERICAN DREAM

It's the dream of all British musical artists – to crack America. The land of Hollywood, glamour, skyscrapers and enormous wealth is an irresistible prospect. No matter that most British acts have failed to make it Stateside, the dream remains as strong as ever. Amy had the advantage that her US campaign caught the attention of the American media. In May 2007, the *Wall Street Journal* published a major feature to coincide with her arrival on those shores. It summed up brilliantly the challenges that faced her and put into context her arrival in the land of the free. However, Christopher John Farley's article was not without its reservations about Amy: 'Though one could argue that given her influences, Ms Winehouse's ascension isn't really evidence of the rise of a new British musical empire, but more proof of the pervasive influence American music and culture have around the world.'

He pointed out that, when he interviewed her, all the acts she name-checked were American: Frank Sinatra, Thelonious Monk, Charlie Parker and Michael Jackson. He argued that what the States were seeing, with the arrival of Amy and fellow Brits Lily Allen and Joss Stone was not a British invasion, but a British echo, in which Brits brought their own take on American music to the American audience. He praised Amy's 'rough, outspoken' personality before concluding, 'The British aren't coming. They're already here – and they may be staying for a while.' Plenty for Amy to feel positive about there, then, even if he insisted on claiming Amy's music as American, in order to offer his approval.

Farley was not alone in seeing a wider trend at force. Writing in the *Chicago Sun-Times*, Mary Houlihan also placed Amy within a grouping: 'A wave of female singer-songwriters from the British Isles are making an impression on fans at home and abroad. What they have in common is a sassy attitude grounded in an irreverent love for updating and mixing popular musical genres.'

Ahead of Amy's performance at the Schubas venue in Chicago, Houlihan singled her out for particular praise: 'This rough-and-tumble performer is the latest to hit our shores. She is a tabloid fixture back home and is definitely a grittier presence than her compatriots.'

The *Fort Wayne Journal Gazette* immediately stepped Amy out of the Brit pack: 'Unlike fellow breakthrough Lily Allen, who sneaks her biting lyrics into smiley bluebeat ska tunes, Winehouse goes for the grit of vintage soul and R&B... Sweet or sour, genuine or just having a laugh, Winehouse is worth spending an hour with.'

Heather Adler, in the *Calgary Herald* wrote,

It seems impossible that such a deep, commanding voice could possibly be mustered by this skin-and-bones, white, Jewish girl, and she might look bored to be doing it at times, but her talent somehow manages to trump all of her trip-ups. Props to Lily Allen and Peter Bjorn & John, too. You kids are good, but you're not 'legend' good like Wino.

A San Francisco newspaper journalist wrote, 'While Allen appears to be a papier-mâché star, Winehouse looks like the real thing.'

Before long, the *Wall Street Journal* was back on the case:

Singing in a smoky voice, Ms Winehouse updates a classic soul sound, complete with trilling horns and drums with a hip-hop edge; her label, Universal, is hoping for a crossover hit. Ms Winehouse's second album has been a big seller in the UK, where it came out in October (her first wasn't released in the US).

The article quoted Universal's international marketing vice president Hassan Choudhury as saying that Amy's success was unsurprising. 'The US is more receptive to UK music than ever before and I put it down to fantastic records and great A&R

from the UK company, having an international view when they sign artists,' he said.

Once again, then, Amy was standing outside the Brit pack. However, the same newspaper was less than complimentary when it came to reviewing *Back to Black*. Noting the album's 'lyrical nods to Ray Charles and Donny Hathaway, not to mention musical rips from Nina Simone', the reviewer sneered,

> Winehouse would clearly love to be viewed as a member of such esteemed and soulful company, but she doesn't come close: In the end, she's too snotty to be sultry, too obvious to be intriguing and too derivative to be of much interest behind her vaguely endearing single 'Rehab', a sad justification for why she doesn't want to clean up her act. Sorry, but the first step is admitting you have a problem.

Ouch!

Amy could afford a smile, though, on scoring the highest new entry by a British female artist in the history of the US chart when *Back to Black* shot in at Number 7. *Back to Black* was enthusiastically embraced by music fans on this side of the pond, entering the *Billboard* Hot 200 chart at an impressive Number 7 and making her the highest debuting British female artist in the history of the coveted US albums chart.

That was followed by similar triumphs for Joss Stone, Lily Allen, Corinne Bailey Rae and KT Tunstall. British female talent had not known the like since Kim Wilde and Kate Bush twenty years earlier.

While it is traditional to see America as an almost impossible nut for British artists to crack – a member of the pop band Busted claimed that statistically one has more of a chance of winning the lottery than cracking America – occasionally Brits can find they are at something of an advantage across the Pond, particularly if their sound is clearly influenced by American music. Industry commentators argue that Americans feel the need to have their own music 'sung back at them' by foreign acts. It reassures them of the worth of the American music scene and is a welcome occurrence whenever it happens.

For instance, it is argued, Eric Clapton's love of the American blues sound was so strong that it outdid any American's devotion to the genre, thus refreshing interest in the blues Stateside. Even more stark was the case of Terence Trent D'Arby, who was presented to the US market as a hot new British act. The truth was that D'Arby was actually a New Yorker by birth, but his record company deliberately chose to market him as a British act because they felt he stood more of a chance that way.

Amy's politically incorrect nature was a breath of fresh air in America, where sanitised goody-goody artists have increasingly ruled the roost. A *San Francisco Chronicle* journalist, Mark Morford, says, 'She should be allowed to march right onto the *American Idol* stage and slap each and every singer upside the head with her huge hair and her wicked sexy tattoos and her mountain of raw British talent, just because. All part of our national rehab, really.' He concluded, 'I think this could be our perfect American model. I think we have the potential.'

Amy is unrepentant about the honest nature of her songs, not regretting this aspect of her songwriting for a moment. 'Not at all,' she said. 'I'm glad that I could be that person. Music is the one thing in my life where I won't ever lie or cover anything up. I could go into a therapy session with a professional, and I would not be as honest as if I had a notepad in front of me. For some reason, when I write stuff I always end up telling the truth, so much more so than in my [day-to-day] life.'

Her friends confirm that just as she is honest and, well, frank in her lyrics, so she is in her everyday life. 'She's a fiery person, but we've never argued,' says John the White Rapper. 'Partly, I'm not that silly, and I know I'd get my balls cut off – if you say something that pisses her off she'll eat you alive – but also because there's never any tension between us. We meet up and chill. It's perfect, really.'

Her frankness, too, was perfect for America, giving her an edge. However, before we get carried away, we would do well to list some of the acts that have *failed* to make it in America. Top of this list must be Robbie Williams, who, in the words of a leading American record company executive, arrived in America by private jet, vowed to conquer the country, and was sent home by bus. Indeed, Williams has yet to come home and is still to be found on the West Coast of America, ruing his spectacular failure to make it there. And what of Oasis, who seemed to implode as a band the moment they arrived in the

US? Although they have since picked up a respectable following there, when they were at the terrifying peak of their fame in the mid-1990s, they were unable to replicate their success in America to any significant degree.

Readers who are interested in not just a graphic example of a band failing to make it in America, but also a cracking piece of television should refer to the MTV series *America or Busted*, which followed the pop band Busted – complete with Amy's friend and former Sylvia Young classmate Matt Willis – as they tried to crack America. At this stage of their career the band were Britain's biggest act and had recently been voted as such. However, in America they faced soul-destroying journeys across the country, to small regional radio stations who mostly turned their noses up at the band. When Busted went busking in Times Square in Manhattan, they were utterly ignored.

Amy's albums were far from ignored in America, though. Both received plentiful reviews in the US press. Many of these reviews were enthusiastic, too. *Frank* tended to be the more reviewed because, as mentioned, the two albums were released in a different sequence in America.

In the *Northwest Herald*, Bryan Wawzenek wrote, 'Where *Back to Black* is sharp, short and sweet R&B, *Frank* is smooth, meandering jazz-pop.' The *Philadelphia Inquirer* added, 'Without the conceptual glue of Mark Ronson's smartly retro R&B production moves, this earlier disc – more stylistically varied and less cohesive – shows Winehouse leaning more toward jazz.'

Said *USA Today*, 'Winehouse fuses her influences with such breezy authority that the songs never sound flagrantly derivative or stale.' The MSNBC website declared, 'Now, just in time to capitalize on the success of the BRITs breakthrough, *Back to Black*, the debut is appearing stateside for the first time. While the latter disc found Winehouse cackling over lush vintage soul backdrops, *Frank* uses sparse instrumentation to achieve a subtler, jazzier effect.'

The *U-Wire Arizona* attempted to put the album into its historical and contemporary context: '*Back to Black* plays as if it is out of the doo-wop era until a track with Ghostface Killah brings the listener back to the need today to feature rappers in music.'

The *Allentown Morning Call* concluded, 'Swinging a mixture of soul, ska and girl-group theatrics, the 23-year-old Brit sounds like she's lived every one of her lyrics.'

Writing in the *Minnesota Daily*, Becky Lang said, '*Frank* is not only good musically, it's somewhat of an anthropological relic for a case study of the triad closest to our culture: copulation, mind-altering substances and parent-offending music. Er, sex, drugs and rock'n'roll.' *Boston Now* gave the album four stars, adding, 'Musically, the CD is laidback, with the band providing sparse, yet tasty accompaniment to Winehouse's vocal stylings. Not without its faults... *Frank* is still an outstanding debut.'

The influential tabloid the *New York Daily News* gave a long and considered thumbs-up. Jim Farber wrote,

It's understandable that Universal Records wanted to introduce the singer to this country not with this sound but with the more instantly accessible *Black*. Now that we're conditioned to Winehouse's persona, and her life, as hovering somewhere between the difficult and the troubled, we're in the right mind to hear a quirkier take on her dazzling talent.

The *Tennessean* praised Amy for taking 'jazz and soul and [infusing] it into a sultry, classy brand of pop that kicks up adrenaline like smashing a crystal brandy snifter'. Not that there was much danger of Amy's getting carried away with all these compliments. After all, one report misspelled her surname as Weinhaus.

As for her live performances in America, they largely went down well, too. Her opening performance in the country came at Joe's Pub in downtown New York. Amy's always been a fan of the city, and of the television show set there, *Sex and the City*. 'I liked the way Samantha would just say anything, tell it like it is. I'm exactly like that,' she says. 'But I'm pretty much like that anyway. I'm not really a product of culture. I've always done my own thing.'

The *Village Voice* voted the increasingly legendary venue the 'Best Excuse to Let a Single Venue Dictate Your Taste'. *Newsweek* calls the club 'one of the country's best small stages' and *New York Magazine* added that 'you never know what you'll find next at Joe's Pub, but you can count on the fact that it will be good, very good.' Charlie Gillett of BBC radio rated it as 'one of the best small music venues I've ever been to'. Alicia Keys, who has performed there, says the artist 'gets all the sweat and the heat from the performances'.

There was heat galore during Amy's performance at the venue, not least because it was a sell-out – a great way to start her American campaign. 'To witness Winehouse is to wonder why art and self-destruction so often dance together,' said one onlooker, adding that she began nervously: 'She makes awkward chitchat in that cockney twang. Tugs distractedly at her trademark ratty do. Yanks nervously on the strapless shift that's sliding dangerously south.' However, she then ordered an amaretto sour, got a hearty laugh and cheer from the crowd for doing so, and then the performance immediately kicked up a gear. 'They keep trying to keep me from drinking, but they forget it's my gig,' she joked, and then launched – appropriately – into 'Rehab'.

The *Village Voice* hailed her as a 'dazzling soul saviour' and *Spin* magazine referred to her 'seductive croon and impressive vocal acrobatics' that 'transformed the venue into a mid-century jazz club'. Universal UK's international marketing director, Chris Dwyer, said the shows 'really got the ball rolling. They were both sold out, had fantastic online and print reviews and everybody was talking about Amy Winehouse in New York when she left.'

Dork Magazine said, 'Fortunately the songs sounded as good, if not better than their studio counterparts. Her stage presence initially let on that she seemed a little nervous. The audience's encouraging shouts, and maybe those amaretto sours she drank, shooed away any butterflies fluttering around in her stomach.' As for Bill Bragin, director of Joe's

Pub, he enthused, 'She's got a great voice; she's got great songs; she's already coming with a larger-than-life persona. She's got all the elements of a star.' The audience included such musical royalty as Hendryx, Citizen Cope and Dr John. Mos Def was also present and wrote his phone number on Amy's jeans backstage and ordered her to call him. Jay-Z also came backstage and raved about *Back To Black*. At the end of the night, Amy summed it up in one word; 'surreal'.

Soon she was to perform at Landsdowne Street in Boston, a 2,000-plus-capacity, multipurpose venue that regularly plays host to both the world's top DJ talent and the world's most popular touring artists. It was one of the first big concerts Amy performed in America. Wearing jeans and white tank top, she performed for about fifty minutes. The *Patriot Ledger's* reviewer said,

> She brought little to no stage presence, appeared heavily inebriated and barely moved around, delivering most of her parts without necessary oomph and often with lazy phrasing. Of the album cuts, only 'Me and Mr Jones' had the room bumping; other ballads, R&B nuggets and hoped-for showstoppers fell flat, despite her smoky delivery.

However, fans who were present gave far more positive reviews of her performance. So too did the *Boston Globe*, which chimed in with,

> Winehouse was so effortlessly, unassumingly herself: no airs, no anxiety, no ingratiating shout-outs to her heroes... The plastic cup from which Winehouse sipped, and then

began to drain, did work a certain magic, as the beverage seemed to go straight to her vocal pipes... Winehouse's tones grew bigger and rounder, her licks wilder.

But the audience seemed restless at times and failed to pay attention to slower, longer tracks such as 'Love is a Losing Game'. (However, that very song was at the same time receiving praise from none other than Prince, who said he was a huge fan of it and hoped Amy would one day join him on stage. Music producer David Gest was also quoted in the press praising Amy, though in somewhat more bizarre terms: 'I would kiss the mole on Amy Winehouse's face and every tattoo on her body, and I'd stick my tongue in the gap where her tooth is missing,' he drooled. 'I love her.')

Soon there was a concert at the Roxy Theatre on the Sunset Strip in West Hollywood. The acts that have memorably performed there include Bruce Springsteen, Nirvana, Tori Amos, Foo Fighters, Guns N' Roses, Al Stewart, Jane's Addiction and David Bowie, and even Jay-Z & Linkin Park have played this highly prestigious venue. Amy's performance at the Roxy drew a celebrity-studded audience – including the likes of Courtney Love, the Strokes' Fabrizio Moretti, Bruce Willis and *Grey's Anatomy* stars Kate Walsh and Sara Ramirez – and she paired a turquoise strapless dress with leopard-print stilettos.

Introducing 'You Know I'm No Good', she told of a time she had betrayed a lover and then told him, 'I do love you', then added, 'But, like, I get bored. I told you I'm no good!' The quip drew a hearty laugh from the crowd. *LA Weekly* said,

Live, Winehouse was noticeably nervous but utterly charming, singing for an audience who knew all the words to all the songs. She was in spectacular voice throughout, backed by a crack band (man, that horn section...) and two chicly attired male backup singers who energetically pulled off synchronized choreography.

Winehouse's own herky-jerky, off-the-beat dancing and ragged emulation of girl-group style somehow underscored an aura of sincerity (a matted beehive with an unkempt tail; an ill-fitting dress that kept sliding down her scary-thin frame; weathered leopard-print shoes rummaged from the back of some tranny's closet). Her awkward performance of femininity befits a woman who can't quite figure how to stop fucking up her relationships and her life.

Celebrity blogger Perez Hilton was in the audience and said, 'She is the stuff of legend, and on Monday night a who's who of hipsters and Hollywood players were treated to a tour de force performance by the "Rehab" chanteuse. You never know if Wino is gonna show up to a gig or if she'll even make it through a show, but she more than held her own at the Roxy.'

And so back to New York. She was interviewed by the prestigious and high-circulation *New York Post* ahead of her two concerts at the Highline Ballroom. The interview took place in the entirely appropriate surroundings of Sammy's Roumanian Steakhouse, a touristy shrine of 'real' Ashkenazi Jewish kitsch. Amy ordered the traditional Jewish dish of chopped liver.

'I'm not ambitious or career-minded. I did an album that I'm really proud of and that's about it for me,' she said. 'The rest of it is all bollocks. I love playing live. That's about it. I wish I could say something more interesting.'

Based on West 16th Street between the Meatpacking and Chelsea districts, the Highline Ballroom opened in April 2007 and has featured such names as Mos Def, Jonathan Brooke, Spank Rock, Meshell Ndegeocello, Talib Kweli, moe., Disco Biscuits and – of course – Amy during its opening month.

Amy was nervous on the night, according to reports. In front of a sell-out audience, including the likes of Talib Kweli, Samantha Ronson and Jane Krakowski, the gig, said the *New York Post*, was 'a drowsy affair because the super-skinny Brit not only has little stage presence, her limited soul style steamrolls her repertoire into flat sameness. One song blended into the next, and her mostly bloodless delivery stood in direct contrast to the music she was singing.' It also dubbed her a 'Stepford Singer' and the best it could bring itself to say was, 'The show was too short to be really awful,' adding that, with 'F**k Me Pumps' and 'Rehab', she was on form.

The *New York Times* also had some criticisms of Amy, but added much praise to the mix. 'The moaning, gliding notes took on an ache or a flamboyance, and the pauses became sly and coquettish or pained. Her spontaneity grew both defiant and playful.' The article concluded on a positive note, saying that, despite her performance being somewhat disappointing, 'her self-consciousness, and the bluntness she has learned from hip-hop, could help lead soul into 21st-century territory'.

Her growing fame in America was leading soul into some strange territories. At designer Patricia Field's birthday party at Manhattan's Cielo, JoJo America of the Ones performed 'Rehab' in drag. Then Amy was quoted discussing US socialite and actress Lindsay Lohan.

'I want to coddle that girl. I really want to hug her,' she said as she worried aloud about the Hollywood party girl to a US magazine. She added the punchline, 'I saw pictures of her coming out of the doctor's and she's crying. She's holding papers in her hand, like, "Oh, it's a note from my liver saying, 'Dear Lindsay, I've gone to Vegas.'"'

Soon, the US media were really buzzing. Indiana's newspaper, the *Star Press*, told its readers, 'Winehouse will seduce you with her voice and suck you in with her wicked words. Don't fight it.' The *Rockford Register Star*'s Melissa Westphal added,

I'm going to need a 12-step program if my obsession with the new Amy Winehouse CD continues. Seriously, folks. I'm talking about a don't-skip-a-track format here. Winehouse tackles love, breakups and exes with humor and a deep, soulful voice that's part blues singer, part '60s girl group lead singer. Let's just say it's more unique than anything you've heard lately.

The leading UK music critic Garry Mulholland has told the author that Amy has – to all intents and purposes – already made it in America. 'As far as I can see, she's cracked America – maybe not every single part of the Midwest but the major cities,' he said. 'She's cracked it – and the big TV shows, too. There's a long tradition of British artists selling American music back to them. That's precisely what she's done so of course they love her.

'It's cyclical. New York and LA and the college towns become obsessed with Britishness – hence "a British invasion". Then people move on and get bored and move on to something else. At this moment we're having a good period in America, whether it's middle-of-the-road things like James Blunt or whether it be edgy things like Lily Allen and Lady Sovereign. What she has, which a lot of those acts don't have but which Radiohead have, hence their success in America, is absolutely inarguable quality.'

However, Mulholland stops short of saying Amy can completely dominate in America. He argues that the level of slogging and sycophancy required to become a mega-artist in America is not something Amy would be well suited to. Quite, the opposite, he argues. 'To break America, the whole enormous country, involves a very great deal of trekking around the whole of America glad-handing anyone who is put in front of you. This is what stops an awful lot of British acts from breaking America because they're not prepared to spend months of their time not playing or writing, just wandering around America sticking their tongues up the arses of minor radio executives. But that's what people are expected to do to become enormous in America. Amy is absolutely un-designed to do that, I can't think of an artist less designed to do that. So, no, she probably won't sell as many records as Garth Brooks, but who needs to?'

Above: The tabloids' favourite couple. With Blake, out and about in Covent Garden.

Below left: Amy performs rather coyly at the Nationwide Mercury Prize Awards in September 2007, where *Back to Black* was up for yet another award: Album of the Year.

Below right: Commercially accessible but always authentic, Amy's music has garnered plaudits from a huge range of admirers. Here she is at the Music of Black Origin (MOBO) Awards at the O2 Arena, Greenwich in September 2007, where she won Best UK Female.

Above: Amy performs during the show at the MTV Europe Music Awards 2007, where, perhaps appropriately, 'Rehab' was nominated for 'Most Addictive Track'.

Inset: A close pal of Amy's is hell-raiser and frequent court-appearer, Babyshambles frontman and ex-Libertine Pete Doherty, seen here arriving at the MTV Europe Music Awards 2007 in November in Munich, Germany.

Below: Amy and hubbie Blake relax in the audience during the show.

Above left: Amy's dad, and staunch support, Mitch, collects keys to her flat from Shoreditch police station in November 2007, during a dramatic period in Amy's personal life.

Above right: Amy arrives with her father at Thames Magistrates Court, east London, to see her husband Blake appear on charges of perverting the course of justice, in November 2007.

Below left: Amy on the way to visit her husband in Pentonville prison, London, December 2007.

Below right: Sporting her dyed-blonde 'do', Amy and her dad go shopping to take her mind off things.

Amy leaves Bungalow 8 nightclub at the St Martin's Lane Hotel after clubbing with Kelly Osbourne and a group of friends.

Songwriter and co-producer (with Salaam Remi) of Amy's second album, Mark Ronson arrives for the XFM New Music Awards held in January 2008.

As her fame and notoriety continue to zoom into the stratosphere, Amy is recognised everywhere she goes. Here she walks down the street with a police escort from a North London shop as a crowd gathers outside.

Amy triumphs in America! Despite not even being in the country, Amy scooped 5 awards at the 2008 Grammys – probably the world's most prestigious music awards. Via a satellite linkup from London, Amy's electrifying performance held the global audience enrapt. With her mum helping her celebrate, she dedicated her achievement to her incarcerated husband, and to London town.

Amy looks a picture of health in St. Lucia. What does the future hold for Britain's greatest living music goddess?

Amy herself would concur with Mulholland's assessment. 'America's a big place. There's a lot of people here that aren't worth insulting. That sounds even worse than saying a direct insult... but there's bad music everywhere. I don't talk about it. I'm very passionate about music, but usually I can be a diplomat and that is what I'll be doing while I'm here – hopefully.'

However, Amy's proudest moment in America was yet to come. The most prestigious music awards there – and arguably the most prestigious in the world – are the Grammys. The Grammys originated in 1957 when top record executives from Los Angeles decided to create an association where recording professionals could be rewarded for their artistic creativity. The Grammys ceremony is the time when everyone in the music industry comes together to commemorate the year's best musical achievements and highlights.

Down the years there have been plenty of memorable moments at the Grammys. In 1971, the Song of the Year, Record of the Year and Album of the Year categories were won by Simon and Garfunkel with *Bridge Over Troubled Water*. The following year saw the first Grammys to be televised and first held in New York. Since then, the broadcast of the ceremony has become a major event in the television calendar. Other years that might have caught Amy's attention include 1996, when her hero Frank Sinatra won Best Traditional Pop Vocal for *Duets II*, and 2004 when Beyoncé Knowles won five Grammys. Other winners in recent years include Red Hot Chili Peppers, U2 and Mary J Blige. It is held at the $375 million Staples Center in Los Angeles.

Given this glittering background and the prestige of the award, Amy was delighted to learn that in 2007 she was nominated in not just one but *six* categories for the fiftieth annual awards, to be held in February 2008. She was nominated in the Record of the Year, Album of the Year, Song of the Year, Best New Artist, Best Female Vocal Performance and Best Pop Vocal Album categories. Amy was the only performer to appear in all four of the most prestigious categories, but she fell short of drawing the most nominations. That distinction went to the rap star Kanye West, who led the field with eight nominations, including his third for Album of the Year for the latest CD in his college-themed trilogy, *Graduation*. Her rivals for the Record of the Year were Beyoncé's 'Irreplaceable', Foo Fighters' 'The Pretender', Rihanna's 'Umbrella' and Justin Timberlake's 'What Goes Around Comes Around'.

Host George Lopez had a few jokes at her expense at the nomination ceremony in Los Angeles in December. 'Could somebody wake her up this afternoon around six [o'clock] and tell her?' Lopez said. 'Usually when I'm high and drunk, I'm not very good, but Amy has it down to where she can get a good buzz going and be very creative. She makes Lindsay Lohan look cool.'

Naturally, news of Amy's sextet of nominations made huge headlines in America and back in Britain. WEST IS BEST, WITH AMY RIGHT BEHIND, screamed the *New York Post*. The *New York Times* wondered aloud whether her 'well-publicized problems raised questions about how Grammy voters would view her'. The *Los Angeles Times* went with, WINEHOUSE IS BUZZ-WORTHY FOR THE

GRAMMYS. The *Canada National Post* ran with, WINEHOUSE VS. FEIST: A GRAMMY SHOWDOWN. Back in England, *The Times* was more sober: AMY WINEHOUSE HAS REASON TO CELEBRATE WITH SIX GRAMMY NOMINATIONS. Most memorable of the lot, though, was the *Village Voice*, which headlined its response THIS YEAR'S GRAMMY NOMINATIONS: FUCKING INSANE. In a less direct way, some at home complained about Amy's nominations, too. Amanda Platell wrote in the *Daily Mail* that, despite Amy's problems,

> Our amoral music industry lionises her. What sort of message does that send out to the singer, and more pertinently, to her many young and impressionable fans? For the music industry so publicly to canonise a self-destructive junkie is to endorse and encourage her nihilistic behaviour.

GRAMMYS MAY BE LIVING DANGEROUSLY THIS YEAR, said *the San Diego Union Tribune*. 'Viewers can expect potential fireworks from West and a possible meltdown from Winehouse, whose very public drug and alcohol problems have made her a tabloid queen in Europe and beyond.' It was also discussed that another of the nominees, Chad Pimp C Butler had died shortly before he received his nomination. So there was plenty for the tabloid press to get their teeth into there, too.

Among those in the American record industry, there was joy. 'Amy Winehouse is incredible. I think she should have got a little more positive recognition,' said singer-songwriter Ne-Yo. Grammy-winning producer John Shanks called Winehouse's album *Back to Black*, which included the telling hit 'Rehab', 'an important record'. Shanks added, 'I don't think her troubles are really going to hurt her. I think the sound of that album made an impact.'

First word from Amy herself in response came via the mouth of Mark Ronson. 'I called her today because the record was something that we went through together... Hopefully she will get into America so we can celebrate. Amy doesn't get excited about anything,' he explained. 'She was never once excited while in the studio. And today she's just like, "Yeah, Ronnie Chops, we got Grammy nominations." That's her. But she's happy and psyched.'

This was followed by the official statement from Amy herself: 'Thank you for all your kind letters and emails, I am grateful for all your support. I'm honoured to have my music recognised with these nominations – this is a true validation from people I respect and admire.'

More than anything, Amy and those close to her hoped that these nominations would remind people that, for all the controversy and discussion that surrounded her lifestyle, Amy remains a musical artist and a supremely talented one at that. 'After a tempestuous year of incredible highs and incredible lows, some people forget that she isn't just a tabloid queen,' said an excited Island Records Group UK president Nick Gatfield. 'She's actually a hugely talented artist. We are all really pleased about the Grammy nominations, obviously. And we hope things will get better from now on. She must keep busy.

'It's a reflection of her status [in the United States] that when you flick through the TV coverage [of the nominations], it's her image they use above everything else,' Gatfield added. 'She's made a bigger impact than even her record sales would dictate.' Not that

Amy should or would be getting carried away. 'Getting so many nods, it doesn't mean your career is going to take off,' warned Giant Step co-founder and CEO Maurice Bernstein, whose music and lifestyle marketing company handled the grassroots outreach for *Back to Black*. 'But this was hands down the best album of 2007. Nothing album-wise has come out that has touched it from start to finish; the quality of sounds, the soul.'

Then came the inevitable discussion about whether Amy would make the award ceremony. The *Charlotte Observer* kicked off the discussion, asking, 'Now that the Grammy nominations have been announced, the big question is whether British songstress Amy Winehouse will actually make it to the awards ceremony. It's looking unlikely unless she gets help soon.' The writer pleaded directly to Amy: 'Don't be like Britney at the VMAs and embarrass yourself at the Grammys. You're more talented than that.'

Those behind the Grammy's were naturally very keen indeed to see Amy appear at the ceremony. 'I'd hate to see technicalities prevent creativity from happening on the stage,' said Neil Portnow, president of the National Academy of Recording Arts and Sciences. 'I think it talks about the strength and the excellence of her music and the way that it's received by our membership.'

Word soon came from Amy that she would of course be attending. The whole Grammys news was music to her ears, because she'd recently had to cut short a UK tour in upsetting circumstances.

On the night, Amy was unable to attend the ceremony due

to visa complications. However, that was not enough to stop her winning five prizes: Record of the Year, Best New Artist, Song of the Year, Pop Vocal Album and Female Pop Vocal Performance. It was a colossally successful evening for her, as she became the first ever British female artist to win five Grammys in one night.

She left rehab for the evening and performed two songs – 'Rehab' and 'You Know I'm No Good' – via satellite from the Riverside Studios in London. Her performances prompted a standing ovation over in Los Angeles and she said: 'Thank you very much, it's an honour to be here. Thank you very, very much.' She also delivered her acceptance speech via satellite, dedicating her success to 'My mum and dad. To my Blake, my Blake incarcerated.

'I am so proud of this album,' she said in reference to *Back To Black*. 'I put my heart and soul into it and it's wicked to be recognised in this way. I feel truly honoured to be mentioned in the same breath as many of the artists present tonight and to win is even more amazing.' She was mobbed by ecstatic band members, friends and family on the stage.

Despite being 5,500 miles away, Amy was the talk of the town in LA. With this latest triumph, her dream of making it big in America came true as the entire nation sat up, took notice and demanded to know more about this remarkable singer who couldn't make it to the Grammys but still won five awards. America is her oyster.

Chapter Nine

NO SLEEP 'TIL BRIGHTON

In November 2007, Blake Fielder-Civil, aged twenty-six, and Michael Brown, aged thirty-nine, were due to stand trial at London's Snaresbrook Crown Court on charges of assault causing grievous bodily harm relating to an incident in June of that year. However, days before that trial was due, Blake was also arrested and charged with conspiracy to pervert the course of justice in relation to the assault case. He was remanded in custody to await trial and, as he was led away in handcuffs, Amy shouted to him, 'Baby, I love you, I'll be all right.' Blake had time to shout back, 'I love you too' before he was pushed into a police car. Both Blake and Michael Brown denied the charges. He was refused bail. 'Amy's totally distraught. She kept saying to me, "I love him. He's done nothing wrong,"' said her mother-in-law Georgette Civil.' She was really upset because she couldn't go and visit him. Amy has told me she'll stand by Blake whatever happens.' Soon, there were six men facing conspiracy charges.

Against this backdrop of pain, uncertainty and controversy, Amy hoped that the UK leg of her European tour would see at least a sense of calm return to her world. Back on home turf, she hoped, she could draw increased wellbeing from her domestic fanbase. It is worth recalling – before we turn to this ill-fated tour – how brilliant Amy can be onstage when she is on form.

Somerset House has been described as 'Britain's first office block, built when Britain suddenly realised it had an Empire, but a capital city that looked like Scunthorpe', by *The Times*, which added that as a concert venue it was 'much too posh for a mosh pit'. Amy performed there in the summer of 2007 and charmed all present. Described as being 'as meek as a kitten' by *Gigwise*, she was certainly in a mellow mood. She confessed to the audience that she 'was not the most organised of people – but I've been looking forward to this gig for I can't tell you how long'.

Introducing a blistering cover of 'Hey Little Rich Girl' by the Specials, Amy gave a cheeky nod to her recent no-shows at concerts, saying, 'This is a song I've been doing when I'm away. That's obviously when I show up for a gig.' She hopped off stage a few times to kiss Blake, who was waiting in the wings. As she announced the final song, 'Valerie', some of the crowd booed her impending exit from the stage. 'Boo you,' she joked. 'I've been here at least an hour and I haven't even collapsed once.'

Caspar Llewellyn-Smith, writing in the *Observer*, acknowledged Amy's relatively punctual arrival on stage and added,

The gig that followed showed her abilities to their very best. She was dressed to the nines and impossibly thin in her checked dress with micro-skirt, and with her massive back-combed beehive which, one often fears, will topple her over. And yes, she was slightly crazed and tired, at times, and emotional, possibly. But the real question was: who would want it any other way?

The *Sun* said 'she deserves a champagne reception'. During 'Rehab', Amy had been joined onstage by friend Kelly Osbourne. Amy had indeed been looking forward to these open-air concerts. 'I'm really looking forward to it, because I never went to any festivals when I was younger,' she says of her hefty summer touring schedule. I used to go camping but by the time I was old enough to go to them I wasn't interested any more.'

So, all was well at Somerset House. However, the opening night of the winter 2007 tour at the Birmingham NIA was far from a calm affair, and the press coverage in the ensuing days only added to the sense of controversy and danger that surrounded her. 'It was one of the saddest nights of my life,' wrote the *Birmingham Mail*'s music critic Andy Coleman in his review of the concert. 'I saw a supremely talented artist reduced to tears, stumbling around the stage and, unforgivably, swearing at the audience,' he wrote. He even refused to give the concert the paper's customary star rating, since 'this was a show by a troubled individual that should never have gone ahead'. Harsh words, and yet these were among the kinder conclusions drawn from perhaps Amy's most controversial concert to date.

The drama kicked off when Amy reportedly locked herself in a backstage toilet, prior to her appearance. 'I can't go on without Blake,' she screamed from inside the cubicle. 'How can I live without him? I need him. I need my baby.' According to an eyewitness, 'Her aides and our staff went into panic mode as Amy refused to leave the loo. We could hear her sobbing from outside. She was saying she couldn't go on without Blake. It made everyone worry she would do something stupid to herself. Eventually, aides convinced her to come out and that everything would be OK, but it was touch and go for a while.'

Then Amy finally took to the stage, wearing a see-through black top and a miniskirt. She was more than half an hour late and some in the audience had already grown restless and frustrated while waiting for her. A slow handclap had started up minutes before she took to the stage. Some started booing her. Introducing 'Wake Up Alone', she told the audience, 'This is for my husband.' As the song ended, she said, 'Nothing's going to bring my husband back.' As the performance became increasingly shambolic, more members of the audience turned on her, with heckles and boos being thrown. Shocked, she said, 'Let me tell you something. First of all, if you're booing you're a mug for buying a ticket. Second, to all those booing, just wait till my husband gets out of incarceration. And I mean that.' She then added that the audience were 'monkey c**ts'.

Also during the set, she dropped her microphone and stumbled into the guitar stand. Finally, she seemed to shed tears prior to singing 'Valerie' and then walked out before the song had finished. By this time, it is reported, hundreds of fans had already walked out of the venue in disgust. Some of them were demanding refunds. The tabloid press had descended like vultures to the venue, many of their number openly wishing for some tragedy and drama in the evening. There was plenty of that on stage and some of it off. A tattooed, cross-dressing stalker turned up to the venue, promising to follow Amy everywhere on tour to 'take care of her'. He was evicted, yelling, 'I can take care of her now that Blake isn't around. I love her.'

Many of the more normal fans were quoted in the press during the following days. One said, 'She came on stage half an hour late. She managed four songs but was slurring her words and swaying all over the place. It was atrocious. The song dedicated to her husband was so bad it was like swinging a cat round your head.'

Another moaned, 'Her singing was awful, out of tune and slurred. She sang for around fifty minutes – drinking throughout. I have never seen so many people leave a show. "Valerie" was my favourite song – she massacred it!'

Kinder sentiments were forthcoming, though. One fan, Zoe Giorgio, said, 'When she did sing she sounded phenomenal but she was not ready to be up on that stage. She was so weak, so vulnerable.' Another fan said, 'If my husband was in prison I wouldn't have the bottle to stand up on stage and do that, so I think fair play to her I really do. Her fans should support her.'

They should indeed. It must be asked what these disgruntled fans expected when they bought their tickets to the show. As Helen Brown wrote in the *Daily Telegraph*,

> The 24-year-old's troubles have been fodder for months now. She has been photographed drunk and bloody. She cancelled shows due to 'health issues' and confessed to chemical addictions, bulimia and bipolar disorder. Then this week her husband, Blake Fielder-Civil, was arrested.
>
> If the 'appalled fans' had bought their £20 tickets to see a slick, wholesome pop show, they'd have had cause for complaint. But they can't pretend that was the case. Whatever else Winehouse might be accused of, the self-proclaimed 'ugly drunk' can't be charged with mis-selling herself. She lives a life of high drama. And she has used that troubled experience to create an excellent album's worth of highly dramatic songs about desperate love, alcohol addiction and drug smoking. Her 'appalled fans' must have heard them or they wouldn't have paid for tickets.

This author, too, supported Amy, writing on the *Guardian* website,

> She's for some time been well known to miss concerts, or

arrive late and inebriated. So when fans flocked to her shows in the hope of some in-the-flesh experience of her drunken and shambolic lifestyle it seemed extraordinarily hypocritical of them to complain when – gasp! – her shows turned out to be drunken and shambolic. Some of them asked for refunds, too. I wonder how they argued their case? They couldn't cite the Trade Descriptions Act, surely, because as she veered between genius and disaster, Winehouse kept her end of the bargain impeccably every night.

This contradiction of concertgoers' expectations seems peculiar to her. Pete Doherty has long been a less than reliable live prospect but manages to get off far more lightly. And when Shane MacGowan was routinely late and drunken onstage he seemed if anything to gain extra kudos among most of his fans. After all, as much as they'd gone to sing along to 'Dirty Old Town', they'd also pitched up in the hope of seeing a train wreck.

In any case, since when did we want our artists to be so predictable, tame and clean-living? I'm far more worried about the stars who don't stagger down the road at 5 a.m. dressed in their bra. Winehouse will be back next year. To those who booed her, I suggest that if they want a Leona Lewis, they go and see Leona Lewis.

Andrew Lloyd Webber was, somewhat surprisingly, a member of the audience and the music impresario was impressed with her performance, which he said 'showed flashes of genius with an Ella Fitzgerald quality'. To him, the reports of a disastrous performance were strange. 'I thought there were moments when she was absolutely magnificent,' he explained. 'I didn't notice her doing anything peculiar. I thought her voice was toned and she was handling material you would not expect a girl of her age to cope with.'

He did, though, notice the negative response of some audience members. 'It was strange what happened. Suddenly, way into the show, the audience suddenly turned on her and she wasn't equipped to handle it. I was with Sir David Frost and he has seen it all. Neither of us could work out why the crowd turned on her – it just happened in one moment.'

Rounding off his rallying support for Amy, he said, 'She is a big star and the awful thing about it is she's going to be crushed like a butterfly and it's not right. That girl needs to be nurtured and helped through all of these problems because she is a major, major talent. I'd say there's an Edith Piaf quality to her, which is very rare. She lives those lyrics.'

There were also words of support from the band Girls Aloud. Nadine Coyle said, 'Amy Winehouse is just such a talent. Her voice has brought something back that hasn't been around for decades.' Sarah Harding chimed in with, 'Isn't it weird that the really talented people always seem to crumble under that kind of artistic pressure?' Cheryl Cole added, 'She's absolutely amazing, but it's a shame that her personal life overshadows the talent.'

Amy's old teacher, Sylvia Young, wrote an open letter about Amy at this point. It read,

I have followed Amy's career closely from the time she left the school and continue to do so. I am delighted that she has become a singing sensation and, even at such a tender age, has achieved so much.

I love her 2003 debut album, *Frank*, made when she was just 20, and her debut single, 'Stronger Than Me', won an Ivor Novello award for songwriting.

Equally I enjoyed her *Back to Black* album, released in 2006. At first I was sanguine about her erratic behaviour. I thought she was just a wild child enjoying life to the full, I had no idea it would escalate so much.

It appears that Amy wants to be free to do whatever she chooses. I have only ever felt as concerned about one other ex-pupil, Danniella Westbrook, at the height of her troubles.

She starred in *EastEnders* but became a cocaine addict with terrible results. Yet she has fought her way to a complete recovery and I am truly proud of her. She is the most courageous girl I know.

I am hoping that Amy's superintelligence will give her the confidence to draw back, too. It is her choice which path to follow but I want her to choose the right one and move on soon. I want her to become a legend – but in her lifetime, not after.

If I met her today I would give her a big hug and say: 'My dear Amy, you were never expelled. Instead you were admired and loved, as you are today. Please try to harness these feelings to help you get back on track.

I know how hard you can be on yourself. I also remember that you don't like being told what to do. But think back to the time when you wrote that what you really care about is people hearing your voice.

All of us who care about you want you to fulfil your unique destiny.

Also, in Amy's defence, it must be remembered what stresses she was under at this point. She had spent the afternoon visiting Blake in prison – and had her beehive searched on the way in! – and was utterly distraught by the experience. A friend of hers insists that Amy 'wasn't drinking before or after the gig and stuck to Lucozade all night'. Frankly, even if she was drinking before the gig, only the coldest heart could blame her for doing so after she'd gone through the horrific experience of visiting her husband in jail and having to leave him there and perform at a concert in front of thousands of expectant fans.

Lloyd Webber's words were balanced, considered and fair, which is more than could be said of the media storm that descended upon Amy in the wake of the Birmingham concert. Scenting blood, the press reported that her tour manager had quit. Thom Stone found traces of heroin in his system from, he claimed, passively inhaling the fumes when Amy and Blake took drugs. He showed Amy a doctor's note warning her that the pressures of being her tour manager had been ruining his health. 'He was constantly bailing her out,' said a source. 'He was watching them get off their head on drugs and wondering whether Amy was even going to get up on stage. It was a nightmare job.'

In the heady atmosphere of the week, this was reported as a major setback for Amy. However, as someone close to her revealed, she was far from disappointed at her tour manager's resignation. 'When he produced this note, Blake and Amy thought it was a joke. They didn't get on with Thom and were taking the piss when he tried to pull that excuse to leave. They wanted rid of him anyway.'

By this stage, though, the media were relentless in their suggestion that Amy was on the brink of suicide. *The London Paper*'s front-page headline was typical: AMY ON THE BRINK OF MELTDOWN. The paper's story reported that 'a bedraggled Amy Winehouse left her north London home early this morning amid fears she was on the brink of a meltdown.' Not that journalists were the only people feeling concern towards Amy. Fans on the forum of her official website discussed a rumour that she had died from a drug overdose.

There were also profound fears for Amy much closer to her home during the same week. In the early hours of the morning, Amy's parents called an ambulance to her house, amid fears that she might be on the brink of suicide. A source said, 'Amy's family are petrified she'll do something stupid. They know she's very low at the moment and misses Blake terribly. They were trying to reach her on the phone yesterday evening and they were also trying the flat in Hackney where she's been staying but they couldn't get in touch with her. They immediately feared the worst and called an ambulance and police to go and check on her. But, thankfully, Amy showed up and was fine.'

Indeed she was fine, as her brother Alex confirmed during an interview with GMTV, in which he attempted to bring some sanity to the increasing madness of the media's coverage of Amy. 'I spoke to her last night. She told me to give her cats a kiss. She sounded fine, definitely,' he said. He said that he had tried to get her to mend her partying ways but said that he hadn't been able to get her to listen. 'When I've tried to say, "What are you doing?" it just ends up in an argument. However, I know that she has a voice in her head saying, "Calm down",' he said. Alex concluded, 'She wanted me to say that she loves Blake, because he's watching.'

Meanwhile Janis spoke out, too, saying, 'My heart goes out to her. She's under immense stress over Blake's imprisonment. I wouldn't hesitate to tell her to pull out if I feared she was in danger. I don't want Amy destroying herself. But I think she will get by and come through what is a terribly lonely time for her right now.' She also blamed Blake for Amy's woes, saying, 'Everyone else can see it, but Amy chooses not to. I think he introduced her to them [drugs] and now she thinks, "Oh, this is good, this is OK." I think she's still a child. Personally, I think it's overtaken her a bit.

'I step back, look at life and think, "Well, they've put him away." I can see life taking care of the situation. I was more worried when they were together. I think, while they're apart, she'll wake up and think, "What have I done?" Again, it's a sense of fate. Thank God he's gone inside, because it's also a case of now he's going to learn.'

And so to Scotland, for the second date of her UK tour. As a spokesman for the Glasgow Barrowlands venue was expressing concern over whether Amy would show up for the concert – 'There is a worry that she will not front with everything that's going on,' he said; 'it would be a tremendous shame if she didn't play' – Amy was boarding a flight to Glasgow. She reportedly nipped into the toilets for a crafty smoke, prompting a bitchy announcement over the intercom from one of the flight crew. 'Our famous little friend is smoking in the toilet,' said the air hostess. 'It's just that the smoke alarm hasn't gone off yet.' A fellow passenger said Amy seemed to be under the influence of something. 'She was lolling in her seat and looked totally out of it. She kept locking herself in the toilet. Other passengers were having to troop to the other end of the plane and were getting annoyed.' After disembarking at Glasgow Airport, Amy became annoyed with her security guard. 'What the fuck is this airport all about?' she screamed at him.

There were screams, too, as she took to the stage at Glasgow Barrowlands later that night. The audience gave her a deafeningly warm welcome and the relief on not just her face but those of her band was clear. Wearing a stunning silk dress, she told the crowd, 'This is the second night of the tour but it feels like the first. I love you, Glasgow.' Once more, she dedicated 'Wake Up Alone' to Blake and said, 'This song is for those people who are lucky enough to wake up every morning with the person they are in love with. This one's for my husband. I love you. I love you, too, Glasgow.'

As she introduced the closing number, 'Valerie', she said, 'I might not be able to be with my Blake in a minute. But let me tell you something: my husband is the best man in the world.' As she took her much-deserved bows, she paid tribute to the crowd, saying, 'Thank you so much for having us. I mean it, and I'm sorry I was late.'

The following night's performance at the Barrowlands was also well received, with one fan describing it as 'flawless and fantastic'.

Could this performance herald a calming in the media coverage of her? No chance, especially as a video was uploaded to YouTube which, it was claimed, showed her snorting drugs during a concert performance. The footage shows her retrieving something from her beehive and holding it near her nose. It was taken during her performance at Zurich in October. The conclusion that she must have been taking drugs onstage was reached too quickly. She could just as easily have been wiping her nose with a tissue; the footage is inconclusive. At least the *Sun* managed to get a clever pun out the episode, asking: Is AMY MIS-BEEHIVING? The same newspaper also claimed that, as the tour bus left Glasgow, some clingfilm wrapped in burnt foil was thrown out of the window.

Then news broke that a sixth man, Michael Brown, had been charged with conspiracy to pervert the course of justice in connection with Blake's case. However, with Blake incarcerated, some of those close to her were keen to try to move her away from him.

'Her friends are trying to pull her the other way now she's

no longer under his influence,' said one. 'A number of them are over the moon he's been locked away as it gives them a chance to work on her – but she seems determined to stick by him. Her father Mitch is keeping an eye on her as she's so vulnerable at the moment and is known for self-harming, so there are concerns for her wellbeing. Her friends and family are worried she might do herself some harm.'

Amy's uncle, Brian Linton, went as far as sending an email to the *Sunday Mirror* saying, 'We are still worried sick about Amy but now there may be a chance to break the Svengali-like hold Blake has over her.'

Blake, meanwhile, was also trying to keep an eye on her, albeit from the confines of prison. During a telephone conversation with Amy he said, 'For the first time in months I've been eating three square meals a day. I feel so much better. But you're taking drugs, not eating and now you're fainting. You've got to eat properly and stop sticking your finger down your throat. Bulimia's taking a terrible toll on you.' There were signs that Amy was ready to take more care of herself when she signed up for a six-month course with a yoga guru. 'She loves the yoga, which is practised to music,' said a friend. 'The idea is it gives you a natural high and takes away the desire to do drugs.'

It was a week for people to come out of the woodwork and criticise Amy, using her troubles for their own ends and pinning their own issues onto her. Even Antonio Maria Costa, head of the United Nations Office on Drugs and Crime, managed to put the boot in, blaming her for poverty in Africa.

'Rock stars like Amy Winehouse become popular by singing "I ain't going to rehab" even though she badly needed, and eventually sought, treatment... A sniff here and a sniff there in Europe are causing another disaster in Africa, to add to its poverty, its mass unemployment and its pandemics,' he said.

While being held responsible for poverty in Africa, Amy was simultaneously the inspiration for a photoshoot arranged with controversial *Big Brother* contestant Jade Goody. So impressed is Goody by Amy that she and boyfriend Jack Tweed dressed up as Amy and Blake for the photos. Goody donned a beehive and had fake tattoos over her arm while Tweed donned a trilby hat, Blake-style.

However, what was ridiculous was the tabloid tale that held Amy responsible for the killing of a hamster, allowing the *Daily Mirror* to paraphrase one of tabloid journalism's most famous headlines, screaming: AMY WINEHOUSE KILLED MY HAMSTER! (This was a nod to a celebrated *Sun* front-page headline of March 1986 that read, FREDDIE STARR ATE MY HAMSTER, a claim later denied by both Starr and Max Clifford, the publicist behind the story.) The story concerns Peter Pepper, a former session musician for Amy.

One birthday, he received a hamster as a pet. He named it Georgie Porgie. As Pepper and Amy sank drink after drink one night, he got Georgie out to show her. Eventually, Pepper went to bed, leaving Amy still drinking. After a while, he got back up and found Amy had drunk the drinks cabinet dry. Pepper, now a member of the band Palladium, who opened for Amy at her Somerset House concert, goes on: 'The next thing I know,

Georgie bites me, runs off and Amy says she'll catch it. I was a bit suspicious when she said she was good with hamsters. Just hours later, the hamster was stone cold and hard. I don't know what she did to it!'

He describes the whole experience as 'particularly traumatic', explaining, 'Not only did I have to deal with a dead hamster, but for some reason Amy had also managed to unplug the freezer and flooded the whole kitchen and utility room.'

Sounds like a great night!

Another great night was her next stop on the tour. In Newcastle she appeared on stage forty-five minutes late, apologised 'from the depths of my heart' for her lateness and gave a triumphant performance, which was received rapturously by the audience. Crucially, 'she seems to be reconnecting with the simple highs of performing before an audience who love her', wrote reviewer Dave Simpson in the *Guardian*. Having noticed a young girl in the audience with a 'fantastic' beehive haircut, she passed her a present. She also implored her audience to send a present of their own to Blake. 'I'm going to send him a bouquet of flowers. And I want everyone here to send Blake a red rose.' She then gave out his address at London's Pentonville Prison, where he was on remand. After a few drinks with her band, Amy went to stay with an aunt and uncle. They watched *Hot Fuzz* and *Shaun of the Dead*.

It wasn't only family who were lifting her spirits. Babyshambles singer Pete Doherty was also in regular contact with Amy during this troubling period. 'I speak to Amy almost every day,' he said. 'She just wants her man back for Christmas.

They're desperately in love. One good thing is that Blake's got clean since he's been in prison. It's been quite an awakening. Amy stopped doing everything since he went in. She realises how much they have to lose. They're going to lose each other if it carries on. Love, music and melody is the way forward.'

However, Amy had less than glowing words to say about Doherty during Blake's continued incarceration in 2007. 'Why have they given Pete so many chances? It's not fair that my Blake is locked away,' she said. 'I thought they would give him bail, just like they do with Pete.'

Then, she was seen giving a cigarette to a random drunk guy called 'Des', who claimed he had waited for five hours to talk to the singer after he was refused entrance to a club. Amy lent him a smoke, which she signed 'Amy Civil' before boarding her tour bus. As the following day's papers delighted in reporting, Amy appeared to have a white substance around her nose, sparking conclusions that she had been snorting cocaine. WINEHOUSE GOES BACK TO WHITE, said the *Sun*. Meanwhile, the *Daily Mail* quipped, IS IT IMPOLITE TO ASK IF YOU'VE BEEN TO POWDER YOUR NOSE, AMY WINEHOUSE? Then came Blackpool, where she told the crowd of Blake, 'He would have loved to have been here. I spoke to him last night but I can only call either before or after *EastEnders*.' Nice detail.

Two fantastic concerts at Brixton Academy followed. At the start of the first, Amy bounced onto the stage looking full of life. As the opening bars of the set opener, 'Addicted', kicked in, she tried to grab her guitar but the strap was tangled in the guitar stand and a desperate struggle ensued in order for her to make it to the microphone in time for her first verse. This was as close as the evening came to disaster.

However, prior to her third London concert, this time at the Hammersmith Apollo, Amy reportedly locked herself in her hotel room and refused to go to the venue. Her management team spent some time desperately trying to coax her out, with one being overheard saying, 'I can't take this any more. She's a nightmare!' She eventually turned up on the stage an hour late at 10.15 p.m., by which time boos were echoing across the venue and some fans were already demanding refunds.

Fans were quoted as describing the performance as a shambles. 'I paid to see Amy, not some spaced-out girl wandering around,' said one. Another added, 'I've never seen so many people leave a gig early. Get help, Amy.' To be fair, the sentiments aired by fans on the forum of her official website were even harsher. One vowed never to buy a ticket to any acts signed to her record label ever again. The *Daily Mail* slated her appearance, saying her 'smeared make-up, tattoos and a cigarette clenched between her teeth' shocked her fans. It's safe to say that most of her fans would have been aware that Amy smoked and had one or two tattoos on her body, so their shock would presumably have been minimal at best.

At least Amy could console herself with the news that the leading US magazine *Entertainment Weekly* had voted her the 'most buzzed-about star'. Meanwhile, 'Valerie' spent its nineteenth week in the Top Forty, retaining its position at Number 5. She also found an unlikely ally in the lead singer of the rockers Queens of the Stone Age. During the closing stages of the band's concert at Brixton Academy, frontman Joss Home interrupted the song 'Feelgood Hit of the Summer' thus: 'They tried to make me go to rehab, and I said "no, no, no"... because that's the kind of guy I am, baby. "Rehab"? We could hang out on the Thursday, but I'm so busy. I'm so busy with with... nicotine, Valium, vicodin, marijuana, ecstasy and alcohol. We could hang out on Friday, but then there's the...' And then he burst into the song's refrain, loudly shouting, 'C-c-c-c-c-cocaine!'

By now, the press were flocking to Amy's concerts in the hope of further drama or disaster. The best they could do with her next leg of the tour gave the phrase 'scraping the bottom of the barrel' a whole new resonance. They revealed that Amy – shock, horror and hold that front page – caught a taxi home after her concert in Brighton.

'It was really strange,' said an incredulous eyewitness to the drama. 'She appeared to be taking a gentle stroll along the seafront with a friend. Then a cabbie pulled up and they both got in.' But, then, even the most commonplace events in Amy's life have the potential to make headlines. One story in the *Sun* concerned her going to a shop and stocking up on food. 'She was buying bread, cereal, mince, butter, crisps – just the normal things you would stock your kitchen with,' revealed an eyewitness! Turning back to the Brighton taxi episode, as she was due to perform at nearby Bournemouth the following night, the media spoke of the 'mystery' of why she would return to London overnight. Her home is in London and her husband was locked up in prison in London. Not the biggest mystery of the millennium.

The mystery, such as it was, was solved the following day as news broke that Amy had cancelled all remaining concerts and public appearances for the remainder of 2007, after her doctor advised her to take a complete rest. 'I can't give it my all onstage without my Blake. I'm so sorry but I don't want to do the shows half-heartedly. I love singing. My husband is everything to me and without him it's just not the same.'

The concert promoters Live Nation followed up, saying,

Amy Winehouse has cancelled all remaining live and promotional appearances for the remainder of the year on the instruction of her doctor. The rigours involved in touring and the intense emotional strain that Amy has been under in recent weeks have taken their toll. In the interests of her health and wellbeing, Amy has been ordered to take complete rest and deal with her health issues. Refunds for the remaining dates will be issued from the point of purchase.

Some claimed that Amy was told to quit the tour after she had partied hard for three days and three nights without sleep. However, those close to her say that she had spent those evenings not partying but working – recording her third album.

News of the cancellation also put paid to the more-than-fishy rumour that she had been planning a performance at Pentonville Prison, in front of Blake. Said a friend: 'Amy has been in pieces ever since Blake was arrested. She can't stand the thought of him being alone in prison and wants to play a show there. She thinks it would be a fitting tribute to him, it would cheer him up and it would also help her cope with being separated from him.'

Amy had left the tour suddenly for a meeting in London. She was reportedly delighted by the cancellation of the tour. A source says, 'She was in a terrible state... She looked awful and had been in floods of tears. She was fragile and weak like an old woman. It was depressing to watch. When the tour was cancelled it was like a weight lifted off her shoulders immediately.'

Her mother Janis was quick to give her seal of approval to Amy's brave decision. 'Amy's got to take the opportunity of getting herself fitter and stronger. She thinks she's strong but she isn't. I hope she uses the chance to fully recover. I hope she'll take it easy for a while and then get back to writing new material. She's got to get herself clean. It's a matter of her personal survival.'

Fans were quick to send Amy messages of support. One wrote, 'We'll miss you for the little while you're out of the limelight, but we know you'll be back and wonderful and better than ever.' Another wrote, 'Do the right thing by your health. You'll come back stronger than ever! We'll all be here for you!' Writing on Amy's MySpace profile, a third said,

I am so glad they finally cancelled it. It is heartbreaking to see her like this. I've been lucky enough to see her live twice this tour (once in Belgium and once in England), but I can honestly say that if it got cancelled right before these gigs, I would have been ok with it. Cancelling has been a good thing to do. I hope she will get better soon. I love Amy with all my heart.

However, in an online debate on the BBC website, one user was less sympathetic, saying,

I think that she's killed her career off now. Fair enough if doctors are telling her that she needs to rest or go to rehab or whatever but saying you can't perform because your husband is in jail is just sheer lunacy. The public don't have much sympathy for [Blake] anyway so cannot understand why she should be so bothered. As far as most are concerned she's probably got a better chance of sorting herself out without him around.

Blake's arrest had interrupted a much-needed rest for Amy over the festive break. Before he had been arrested, it was reported, Blake planned to take Amy to India for Christmas. 'So the beehived singer has agreed to fly to Miami with pals immediately after Hanukkah celebrations with her Jewish parents Mitch and Janis,' said reports. Her hairdresser Alex Foden confirmed this: 'Amy told me Blake wants her to go away for Christmas to get away from it all. She's not on top of the world. But speaking to Blake on the phone helps. She'll go to Miami if Blake keeps going on about it because she loves him and wants to make him happy.'

In the meantime, Amy stayed in London and was photographed on the capital's streets in the early hours of the morning in December. Wearing just her jeans and bra on a freezing London night, Amy appeared confused and worse for wear as she was snapped at 5.30 a.m. wandering the streets of Bow. 'She came out of the house, walked down the drive and wandered around on the pavement for a bit,' said a local who witnessed the episode. 'She looked upset and agitated, but there was no obvious reason for her to have come outside. It was weird.'

Amy's camp put out a statement trying to stem the tide of hysteria that was increasingly surrounding this fragile young woman:

Amy had been asleep and heard a noise. She went outside to investigate. She didn't realise the time. She was not on an all-night-bender. She heard all these noises, and she went outside to look and there were all these photographers... of course she looked startled. In light of recent reports, it's easy to make false assumptions, but she's getting better and she needs the space to do that.

Paolo Hewitt has some sympathy for Amy, who he believes would have had a far more pleasant ride with the press had she been born several decades earlier. 'Bob Dylan was probably doing just as much gear as Amy but the press just weren't on it,' he says. 'The Beatles and everybody were going ballistic but there was a gentleman's agreement that you didn't report that side of things. When Hunter Davies wrote about the Beatles in the sixties, although there were orgies of debauchery going on, none of it surfaced in the biography because you just didn't report that kind of thing. Amy is unfortunate in that she lives in a media-obsessed age. If she'd have come along in the 1960s, we'd just be talking about her music. That's what's been lost because of all this media attention. Instead, it's "Amy Winehouse the drug addict" and "Amy Winehouse the broken wife of Blake Fielder-Civil". It's not "Amy Winehouse, what a fucking great artist!" I think that's a shame.'

However, Hewitt's sympathy is not without reservations. He wonders whether she has more of an active role to play in all the drama than people might believe. 'She has contributed to that. I don't think she's completely innocent in all of this. I wonder how it is that a photographer happens to be there at half-five in the morning as she emerges from her house in her bra. I don't get that; how did that happen? She seems to be very complicit in this. It's like the fight her and Blake had at the Sanderson Hotel. If you're going to have a fight, have it at home with the doors shut. This playing her dramas out in public is not a healthy thing. It detracts from what is important, which is her music.' Mark Simpson, asked by the author if he believes Winehouse engineers her troubles for publicity, said: 'If they are engineered, then she deserves much more sympathy – and respect – than if they were unplanned.'

She may have looked upset as she stumbled around Bow, but she had decided to move home to that neighbourhood after concluding that her previous home in Camden had too many bad memories, including a drug overdose and numerous memories of Blake. During the move, a 'rather suspicious bag of white stuff' was photographed in the car boot by the *London Lite* newspaper. 'In response to photos published in the *London Lite* of "white stuff" in the back of the car in which Amy Winehouse was driven in, [the items in the bag] are in fact the driver's hand towels,' said a statement from Amy's camp. 'Any implication or suggestion otherwise would be unfair.'

As with the YouTube video, it was obvious to anyone with decent eyesight that the photograph was not of drugs. Once ensconced in her new Bow home, Amy was visited by friends, including Sadie Frost. 'Sadie arrived looking very serious like she was visiting a patient,' an onlooker told the *London Paper*. 'It didn't really seem like a social call.'

The tabloids were by this time running wildly conflicting reports about Amy's health. Some had her in rehab and clean, others had her on drug binges, losing all her teeth. 'Amy is still using drugs when Blake's in prison,' said a source. 'She's using more cocaine and heroin now than ever. She can't stop crying and keeps saying all she wants is peace. She's not eating or sleeping properly and is in pieces.

'Amy is very upset about her teeth because they have literally been falling out,' a source said. 'She has one missing from the front of her mouth, and another one at the back, which is less visible. Her mouth is full of holes and she's desperately worried she's going to lose more. She's actually pulled a tooth out herself, which is absolutely disgusting.'

Only hours before Amy had wandered the streets of London

in her bra, her friend Pete Doherty had dedicated a song to her during a Babyshambles concert in Glasgow. Before the band launched into the anthemic song 'Down in Albion', Doherty said, 'She's a great girl and this song is for her.' Meanwhile, Liam Gallagher of Oasis was also speaking out in her defence. He said, 'She plays with fire, you get burnt. That's the way it goes. If she knows what she's doing's not good then she needs to back up a bit. She's young. I'd probably be doing the same thing – except twice the drugs. I'm sure she'll grow out of it.' Asked about her music, the normally savage and critical Gallagher said, 'It's all right. I like that "Rehab". I've just heard stuff on TV. She's good.'

Liam's hero, the Beatle Ringo Starr, also came out for Amy. 'God bless Amy. She's a great talent and she's going through a situation right now. The good news is that there's more help around now than before.' Then came support from Mary J Blige, who said of Amy and Britney Spears, 'They're human beings, and they're young, in a business that doesn't give a hoot about you. It's just sad. I hate to see any of these females go through it. I was young, and I did dumb stuff – I was doing worse than that.'

Most worried were Amy's parents. Mitchell said, 'I'm very concerned for Amy's welfare. She's very, very tired. She's sorry to have let the fans down. She needs professional help.' Referring to Amy's brother, he added, 'We're a strong family unit and the bond between Amy and Alex is unshakeable. He's always there for her. He's very protective of her and always will be. He doesn't like seeing her hurt or upset. He's upset by the current criticism of Amy, as we all are, and has asked her critics to be a bit more understanding in view of her youth.'

With Blake's imprisonment and Amy's erratic tour performances making the couple an obsession for the tabloid press, it was inevitable that Blake's mother would speak out. It was reported that Georgette Civil said that she was 'delighted' that her son was in prison and also claimed that he too felt it was for the best. 'Blake's more focused now than he has been in years,' she said. 'He's finally taking responsibility for his behaviour, too, and accepts that he and Amy are totally responsible for the mess they're in. Now he's using the time in prison to overcome his drug habit.' She revealed that her son spent his time in prison exercising and reading.

Civil also tried to bring to the public's attention the 'true' Blake. 'Looking at him all dishevelled, gaunt and unkempt, it's hard to remember the bright teenager who won a place at a great local school, who had so much promise.

'It was hugely upsetting to see my son portrayed as some sort of monster who was accused of supplying his wife with heroin and cocaine and I worried terribly that someone would harm Blake as a result. Then there are my two other sons, aged fourteen and fifteen, whose hearts are breaking seeing their big brother being portrayed like this.'

Georgette Civil concluded of Blake, 'He wants her to feel as if they're still sharing life and he's with her every day. Blake thinks that if Amy has a little thing to do for him each day that'll propel her on, give her something to work towards and get her out of bed in the morning.'

Meanwhile, reports of Amy's emotional state varied wildly. One report had her making admiring small talk over *Big Brother* contestant Chantelle Houghton's breasts at a newsagent's. 'Look at Chantelle's tits – I want a pair like that!' Amy is said to have told fellow shoppers.

'Chantelle's boob job obviously made a big impression on her,' a source told the *Daily Star*. 'Amy is desperate to make Blake happy and in her mixed-up mind having a boob op could be just the job.' Mitchell meanwhile reported, 'Amy was visited by a doctor last night. And we're seeing to it that she's monitored very carefully, every single day. So far we're pleased with the way things are going. We're keeping a very close eye on her.'

Which was just as well, if the words of an unnamed friend of Amy's were to be believed. The friend told a newspaper, 'Amy's had her problems but she's really terrified this time. She's teetering on the brink. She's already hatched a suicide pact with Blake. If they're both handed lengthy jail sentences she's determined they'll end it together rather than face years apart. She can't live without Blake. Her family are worried sick.'

The question of Amy's being handed a lengthy jail sentence came about when she was arrested and questioned over the alleged bribery plot on suspicion of which her husband was already in custody. By this time, as we have seen, Blake and five other men had been charged with conspiracy to pervert the course of justice, though denying all charges. Police then turned their attentions to Amy, confiscating her mobile-phone records, bank details and computer software. Officers also visited the singer's accountants, the London-based firm Smallfield Cody, in an attempt to track her financial dealings.

'A twenty-four-year-old woman has been bailed to return to an east London police station on a date in early March pending further enquiries,' said a police spokesperson on Amy's arrest. 'She attended a police station voluntarily and at a pre-agreed time.' A spokesman for Amy said, 'She was arrested but that is common practice for someone being interviewed by police. There have been no charges and she has been released.'

As for Blake, he was said to have been threatened by fellow inmates as part of a kidnap threat against Amy herself. A source said, 'Blake's petrified. He's living in fear for Amy's life *and* his own. At first he thought the guys in here were just trying their luck but the threats have got really bad. He's now under no illusions and convinced they'll go through with what they say.'

The source added, 'They've ordered Blake to pay the hundred grand into a secret bank account within the next few days or else... Amy will be snatched and harmed. She's at her weakest right now, and what with her wandering the streets in the dead of night she's at massive risk. Blake knows it'll be easy to bundle her off in a car without anyone batting an eyelid.'

Amy's life was not made any easier when it was revealed that she had been summoned to appear in a Norwegian court due to her appeal of a fine for marijuana possession. Liv Karlsen, a spokeswoman for police in the Norwegian city of Bergen, explained that this was normal practice. 'If one appeals a conviction, it's the rule that one has to appear in person. So this is not surprising.' Mitchell had already laid out the basis of Amy's defence against this charge during his interview on the *This Morning* television programme, maintaining that Amy had unwittingly signed a confession document written in Norwegian, thinking it was a release form. Police prosecutor Rudolf Christoffersen insisted police were 'very certain the three knew what they were signing and they paid the fine on the spot'.

However, when she next boarded a plane it was not to Norway that Amy travelled but to Barbados, where she took a much-needed break. 'Amy has been desperate to escape England and forget about her troubles for the past couple of months,' said a friend. 'But she didn't want Blake to feel any more alone or abandoned than he already does, so she's waited as long as possible before booking anywhere. Blake's given her his full blessing, as he knows how stressed and out of sorts she's been of late. The plan is for Amy to have a sunshine break, enjoy a few cocktails – and stay away from drugs.

'She's already made a few New Year's resolutions and hopes the trip will become a turning point in her life. Amy wants 2008 to be a year of consolidation and, more than anything, for it to be trauma-free. She's convinced that Blake will be cleared of all charges and is desperate for the couple to enjoy some regular marital stability.'

Other famous people holidaying there at the time included Simon Cowell, Gary Lineker, Michael Winner and Sir Philip Green. A famous name who wasn't in the Caribbean but was positive about Amy at this time was Kylie Minogue. The petite pop legend was asked what was on her iPod and replied, 'A lot of English regulars of the moment, like Arctic Monkeys and the Klaxons. Oh, and Amy Winehouse, needless to say.'

Also coming out in support of Amy at this time was Julie Burchill. She wrote in the *Sun*,

> I love Amy Winehouse, and I'm not at all shocked by her behaviour. We've been used for such a long time to singers who are ambition-led (Madonna and her hordes of pop-tart imitators) that we have forgotten how singers who are talent-led behave.
>
> Edith Piaf, Judy Garland, Billie Holiday – for some reason, and it would take a genetic scientist to explain it, women who have a great talent for singing also have a great capacity for reckless behaviour. Whereas if your talent is a teeny-weeny sickly little thing – see Madonna and mates – then you have to behave the very opposite of recklessly in order to preserve it.

While relaxing in the Caribbean, Amy reportedly decided to renew her wedding vows with Blake once she was back in the UK. 'They're missing each other terribly,' said a friend. 'Amy wants them to repeat the same vows they took when they originally tied the knot in a £60 ceremony in Miami last May.'

Chapter Ten

ONWARDS AND
UPWARDS?

Predictions of Amy's future normally centre on one of two paths: a magical musical comeback, or a drug-fuelled sprint towards an early grave. Those closest to her know that a third way is just as likely. Once, during an interview, Amy was asked to describe herself in five words. She replied, 'Driven, motivated, easygoing, maternal, alcoholic.' She added, 'I'm very maternal. In my circle of fifteen close friends, at least ten of them call me Mum. They text me and say, "Mummy, are you coming out tonight?"'

But maternal Amy wants to be a mummy to more than her friends. She is keen to have children of her own. She says, 'While I love music, I'd really love to have a family, and that's the most important thing to me. That doesn't mean I'm ready to start one right now, as I think I've got another album in me. In the long term I have more family plans. I've got to a point where I've made an album which I'm proud of. Now I need to follow that up, but to have kids as well. Then go to Vegas, open my own casino and perform there every night!'

More maternal muttering was forthcoming when she was asked where she sees herself in 10 years time. 'Well, I'll have at least three beautiful kids,' she replied. 'I want to do at least four or five albums and I want to get them out of the way now. And then I want to take ten years out to go and have kids, definitely. I never used to be broody, but then I realised that I'm turning into a soppy bitch. Goodness in life comes from a sense of achievement and you'd get that from having a child and putting it before yourself.'

She dreams of parenthood and of further albums, but more important than either of these aspirations for Amy must be regaining a sense of control over the chaos that has engulfed her life. With her drink and drug issues, together with Blake's incarceration on remand, 2007 saw her challenged on many fronts. However, 2008 was to be just as dramatic for Amy and her husband. The central act of the drama came in July, when Blake and his friend Michael Brown both admitted grievous bodily harm and perverting the course of justice. Blake was sentenced to 27 months by the judge, who told him: 'In joining in that attack by kicking out at Mr King after he had already been both punched and kicked by Mr Brown you behaved in a gratuitous, cowardly and disgraceful way'.

Amy was not present at Snaresbrook Crown Court for the

sentencing, but she had already offered her own commentary on the case in a typically bizarre manner. When she appeared at Nelson Mandela's 90th birthday party at Hyde Park, she took to the stage to one of the loudest cheers of the night, and performed 'Rehab' and 'Valerie'. She then left to more rapturous acclaim. But it was never going to be as simple as that. When she returned to the stage at the end of the night, to lead the entire ensemble through the Specials' iconic hit 'Free Nelson Mandela', she gave the lyrics her own personal twist. 'Freeeee, Blakey my fella,' she sang over the chorus at one point. Jaws dropped across the park. Reaction was divided between those who thought it was little short of obscene for her to compare her drug-addled husband with one of the finest figures in human history on the occasion of his 90th birthday, and those who thought it was a moment of typical cheeky genius from Amy, whose wit had always equalled her musicianship.

She then performed at a series of festivals, including Glastonbury, the Oxegen Festival, V, and T In The Park. During the course of these shows Amy served up her increasingly familiar live-performance cocktail: the wonderful, the weird and the wasted. The most dramatic moment came at Glastonbury when she appeared to punch a fan in the front row of the audience. 'You don't even know how happy I am to be here tonight,' she had earlier told the audience. Her happiness had clearly subsided when she lashed out at the fan. She topped off the night by spitting chewing gum into the crowd and calling rapper Kanye West a 'c**t'. Thank you, and good night.

This was almost the last that live audiences were to see of Amy for a while, because she had by this stage been diagnosed with emphysema according to her father. 'Theres a small amount there which hasn't gone too far and it's completely repairable,' said Mitch. He added that she would therefore be taking a break from live performances once her contractual obligations had been fulfilled. Mitch, who had by this time become something of a celebrity himself, was trying his hardest to bring some serenity into his daughter's life.

Meanwhile, Amy was once more appearing in media polls, both positively and negatively. For instance, she appeared in the *NME*'s 2008 Villain of the Year poll, but also in the same title's Best Solo Artist and Best DVD polls. *Glamour* magazine named her the third-worst dressed British woman, but then *Sky News* viewers named her the second-greatest Ultimate Heroine. She had topped the voting among viewers under 25 years old. These polls are a mere selection of those she graced, and reflect perfectly the 'love her or hate her, you can't ignore her' position Amy occupies in the public psyche.

Her relationship with Blake has always been a mixed bag, too. When he was released from prison in November 2008, he checked straight into rehab in Surrey. Far from rushing to see him, Amy was instead photographed out and about in London, up to her normal late-night jolly japes. She failed to see him at all during his first month of freedom, even when he launched an (unsuccessful) bid to appeal against his conviction. The grapevine was soon abuzz with rumours that she was in the process of divorcing Blake. 'It's over. There's no way back for us now,' Amy is said to have told friends. 'It was never going to last. I fancied him like mad, like no one else I've ever known. But it's not enough, is it?' Amy would have to travel far and wide to find anyone who believed she should stay with Blake. Soon after she prepared to dump Blake, he reportedly admitted in a taped interview to *News of the World* what many had long suspected: that he introduced Amy to hard drugs.

'I introduced her to heroin, crack cocaine and self-harming,' said Blake. 'I feel more than guilty. The first time Amy took crack she asked me, "Can I try a bit of that?" Crack is the nastiest drug. It makes you paranoid, unreasonable, edgy and totally suspicious of everyone.

'And you can get hooked on it straight away. But I was weak and an addict and I let Amy take some. I didn't stop it from happening. For that I take full responsibility. It became something we did as well as heroin. And then our lives fell apart.' It is to be hoped both parties can rebuild their lives – separately.

As Blake made this confession, Amy was once again in hospital, her fourth hospitalisation in 2008. It had been a strange year for her, during which her immense musical talent and the magnetic charm of her best live performances became secondary concerns. What she instead became known for was her ability to spark negative press stories about her painfully thin body, her drink and drug use and other controversies. Things got so wild that at one point her father Mitch attempted to have her sectioned to a mental institution. With the media following her every move, Amy seemed to many to be on an unstoppable downward spiral.

Where was the music among all this chaos? It was there for anyone who cared to look beyond the 'shock horror' of the tabloids. Back To Black continued to shift throughout the world, with its 11million-plus sales contributing to her topping the charts in the United States. A deluxe version of the album was released in the UK and quickly topped the charts here, too. Back To Black is one of the top ten bestselling albums of the 21st century and royalties from its sales constitute a large slice of her estimated £10million personal fortune. Whatever problems she has in her personal life, Amy has no trouble shifting albums.

Nor in gathering serious musical awards. In May 2008 she was once more nominated for a prestigious Ivor Novello award, and once more she was triumphant. She won the award for Best Song Musically and Lyrically for 'Love is a Losing Game'. Amy was also nominated in the same category for 'You Know I'm No Good'. Organisers said that it was the first time that an artist had been twice-nominated in the category since the awards began in 1955. Mitch accepted the award on her behalf, saying: 'I don't know what I'm doing up here. Amy unfortunately couldn't make it but she's getting better and she sends you all her love.' As it turned out Amy could make it, and arrived – fashionably late – during her father's acceptance speech.

That triumphant evening did little to dispel the media witch-hunt against Amy. Perhaps the only way she will be able to cool their ardour will be to bounce back with some cracking new material. Her record label has been duly encouraging her to deliver a third album. Universal Music Group chairman Lucian Grange says the early samples of material he has heard are extremely promising. He said: 'I've heard some demos and I've heard some simple acoustic songs that she's played me in my office on acoustic guitar. What I've heard has been sensational I'm an optimist and I believe in her. I believe in her as a person and I certainly believe in her as an artist and that's what I hope for.'

As do all Amy's fans, who were greatly cheered as Amy appeared to turn a corner as she partied in St Lucia at the turn of the year. Having spent several weeks drug-free, she flew to the island just before Christmas and stayed there for several weeks. It turned out to be a headline-grabbing sojourn but mostly for good reasons. Amy looked a picture of health as she took trapeze lessons and put on an impromptu circus show for her fellow tourists. She also performed at the hotel bar in the evenings, playing piano and singing for the guests. Also included in her holiday repertoire were a topless balcony boogie and an hilarious impressions of a horse.

She was keen to share her joy. Not only did she spend tens of thousands of pounds flying out friends to join her on the island, she generously splashed out thousands more on meals and drinks for strangers. Her dark relationship with Fielder-Civil seemed a distant memory as she was photographed basking in the sunshine on the arm of a hunky former rugby player. It all looked great fun and seemed to represent a much-needed fresh start for Amy. 'I've finally escaped from hell,' she told a reporter. 'Before I came out here I looked at a photo of myself in the paper and was horrified. My skin was a spotty mess and I was so pale and skinny. I thought "Girl, you've got to sort yourself out or you'll be dead soon". I was depressed, doing drugs and had no life in me at all. Coming here has changed everything. I don't need drugs.'

While reflecting on these facts as she looked out into the Caribbean ocean, Amy noticed a six-foot wave crash against a boat. The impact caused a woman to be flung overboard from the boat, landing among some rocks. Amy immediately rushed to her aid as the woman was in agony and in danger of being swept to her death. Amy carried her to safety and then washed and dressed her wounds. The doomsayers love to predict an early death for Amy. Yet there she was, happy and healthy and saving the life of someone else. To those who know the caring 'Jewish mumma' side of Amy best, her heroics came as little surprise. Long may her new-found health and happiness continue.

DISCOGRAPHY

Albums

Frank	Island, 2003
Back to Black	Island, 2006

Singles

'Stronger Than Me'	Island 2003
'Take the Box'	Island 2003
'In My Bed/You Sent Me Flying'	Island 2004
'Pumps'/'Help Yourself'	Island 2004
'Rehab'	Island 2006
'You Know I'm No Good'	Island 2006
'Back to Black'	Island 2006
'Tears Dry on Their Own'	Island 2006
'Valerie'	Island 2007
'Love is a Losing Game'	Island 2007

Alexandra – A Star Is Born
Chas Newkey-Burden

A soul-singing sensation and inspiring testimony to the rewards of perseverance, Alexandra Burke is the most exciting musical star to emerge in the United Kingdom for many years. This revealing biography chronicles how she rose from a childhood sharing her bed with her sister in a cramped north London flat to winning *The X Factor* and romping to the top of the charts.

Alexandra faced countless obstacles including the wrath of jealous classmates and the heartache of her parents' separation when she was just six. She overcame everything and by the time she was a teenager she had sung on-stage to live audiences, to primetime BBC1 viewers and down the telephone to an impressed Stevie Wonder.

Then came her *X Factor* journey that saw her reach the final seven of her category in the 2005 series before being sent home by Louis Walsh. Three years later she entered the show again and sailed to the final where she was crowned the winner. Chas Newkey-Burden paints a compelling portrait of an inspiring girl who never gave up.

ISBN 978-1-84454-810-1

John Blake Publishing Ltd

Coming Soon

Now you can buy any of these other books by Chas Newkey-Burden from your bookshop or direct from his publisher.

Free P+P and UK Delivery (Abroad £3.00 per book)

Great Email Disasters
ISBN 978-1-84454-410-3   PB   £7.99

Paris Hilton – Life on the Edge
ISBN 978-1-84454-457-8   PB   £9.99

To order simply call this number: +44 (0)207 381 0666

Or visit our website www.johnblakepublishing.co.uk

Prices and availability subject to change without notice